PLATINUM PUSSYCAT

CHRONICLES

THE HEALING JOURNEY OF A SUPER JUICY GIRL

NÉNETTE ADELIZA

FIRST EDITION

Edited by: Speak Write Play, LLC

Design: Ithan Payne Creative
& Jeffery Burns
Cover Illustration: Daniel Flores

www.thesuperjuicygirl.com

Library of Congress Cataloging-in-Publication Data has been applied for.

ISBN: 978-0-578-85621-6

To my dear friend, Vanessa Lipske, who encouraged me to write this book. It is not what we initially thought it would be, but it was necessary. For my sisters who taught me so many life lessons along the way. And above all, with tremendous gratitude, I honor the women of wisdom and strength who were most influential in my life. Your love is the anchor that held me steady on my healing journey. I call your names: my mother Peaches, Aunt Debbie, Wendy Bell, M.D., Mama Lynn, Mama Dee, Aunt Juanita, my Delta mother Clare, Deb King, and my beautiful Aunt June. I dedicate this book to all of you.

Author's Note

Breathe Girl! You can find the courage to love despite the bullshit! I told myself this often when I wanted to give up on love. The good things you deserve are out there, be courageous enough to be vulnerable even when that fight, or flight response comes upon you, and you want to quit and run for the hills. Put the matches back in your pocket, and don't burn down that damn bridge. Light your path instead to find love and restoration.

This book is a memoir. It reflects my recollections of my experiences that I wanted to highlight for the purpose of my healing. Some names and characteristics have been changed, some events have been compressed, and some dialogue has been recreated.

CONTENTS

Introduction

My Truth is My Strength

The beautiful part of my healing journey is how I now courageously display the greatness God created when He made me. I walk confidently as a Super Juicy Girl, in all my glory, with no apologies for my flaws. Loving myself and embracing my "super juiciness" is my way of taking back my power from people who attempted to marginalize my beauty and greatness.

No longer do I feel shame due to my plus size, inner strength, and excellence. I'm unconcerned about how others may throw shade or hate on me because of my innate ability to win. I am here to love myself and my children and receive everything God meant for my life, good, bad, or indifferent.

As early as kindergarten, I possessed a sense of greatness and knew this was because my parents were so awesomely ambitious and driven. I started getting a little juicy around age five. When people said derogatory things about me, I always dismissed their comments because they had no idea who I belonged to. My parents were dope as hell, and I knew people were jealous of them. However, around age nine or ten, something shifted. My parents started taking issue with my size, which caused my confidence to diminish. As a result, I quietly began to second guess myself for the first time. Once this began, it was easier to accept mistreatment from others. I started believing their negative words instead of brushing them off. I know now that this was the initial break in my confidence, which began my trauma around love.

My parents loved me, but they did not show love the way I needed them to, which confused me as a child. As I got older, this confusion about love led me to places I was not supposed to be. I often had to figure things out independently, and I suffered tremendously from this way of socialization. Yes, I survived it all. However, the wounds were deep and painful. My old school parents were physically present in my life, but they had no clue how vital emotional intelligence and health would be for me. My parents had no earthly idea the damage inflicted upon my soul in the name of surviving in this cruel world. Neither did I.

The dichotomy between my professional life and love relationships with family, romantic partners, and friends couldn't be more different. Amid my career success, there was an emptiness that stirred in my soul. I could never put my finger on it, but I masked this feeling of sadness with work and food. After being married for several years, I still did not have children, and it honestly felt like I did not have anything to attach my loving heart to.

Feeling emotionally unsafe with my parents led me to engage in unhealthy relationships with others. As a result, I constantly suffered from a dreadful feeling of not belonging and a deep sense of unworthiness. The more I continued to ignore the emotions; the more numb I became to the pain I was suffering. It wasn't until I heard a devastating confession by my husband that I was forced to put my finger on my wounds and begin to identify how deep the trauma I experienced growing up truly affected my heart and soul.

Before starting my healing journey, I was suffering but did not want to admit that I was stuck in my pain. After reading this book, I want you to know that it is not normal to suffer without trying to heal; you don't have to let people treat you like shit. I hope my story shows you that relationship traumas can manifest in such negative ways that they prohibit you from living your life with love and joy.

Becoming a mother saved my life because it offered me another chance to believe and accept God's love. It was the first time since my childhood that I felt safe opening my heart to someone. No matter how difficult, I knew I had to move and think differently to mend my heart and ensure my child had a fighting chance of living a life filled with love, confidence, emotional intelligence, and a sense of belonging. As a person accustomed to solving problems, having a child compelled me to seek help outside of myself and God, get counsel, and learn how to develop and identify genuine loving relationships.

Once I gathered the courage to face my trauma, I began to love myself completely. On the days when I struggle, I say to myself, "Breathe, girl," and take a moment to push through any negative feelings. From time to time, I may take an entire day or week to pull myself together, and I do so without apology. When I speak, I recognize my voice. I understand what my heart and soul need to thrive, so I nurture and protect my emotional and mental health at all costs. When my soul is stinging from the hurt of someone's attack against me, I address the pain immediately, then proceed to remind myself to trust God for everything.

The Platinum Pussycat Chronicles: The Healing Journey of a Super Juicy Girl is about the relationship trauma I experienced in my life as a young girl and the struggle to forgive myself for trusting people who ultimately chose to betray me. I identify how I confused trauma bonds with love and how these misconceptions impacted my choices in relationships and manifested in negative ways. I share how the two most influential men in my life, whom I thought I could trust unconditionally, turned their backs on me when I needed them the most. Accepting this was the first step I took in my healing process.

The experience of these traumas ultimately led me to trust the greatness I knew I possessed as a child. I hope that being transparent about my pain and trauma will inspire you to face any challenges that may impede you from the happiness you deserve to seek your healing. The process of writing my story has felt like an emergency room visit. When you go to the ER, the hospital staff want you to rate your pain on a scale from zero to ten. The first few chapters of this book start at level ten because they dig deep to reveal and release the root of the trauma that settled in the belly of my soul. By the final chapter, my pain is at "zero" because it ends with the revelation of God's love and me removing the hood of unworthiness that once covered my crown to unveil the masterpiece God created me to be.

CHRONICLE I
WTF DID HE SAY?

What the fuck did he say? That's what I said to myself the night my husband, Brandon, confessed to a level of betrayal that blindsided me and completely sucked all the air from my soul. Unfortunately, it is too familiar for people to find out their partners do things they have no business doing. It could be anything from gambling, spending money secretly, using drugs, drinking too much, to behaving in a way that diminishes their character or the relationship. My husband told me something that night that I would not have imagined in one hundred years. This is how the night began.

As usual, I was in my room watching television while my husband was upstairs in the den with our two-year-old son and my father-in-law. They were watching the NBA Finals, which was one of their favorite pastimes. I'm not sure what came over me. That's a lie; I did know. On this night, I would quiet my mind and be obedient to what God had been trying to tell me for the last few years. Throughout that entire day, God had been speaking to my spirit while at the doctor's office with Brandon's father. Although I was not his favorite person, I invited him to move in with us after suffering a nearly fatal accident. For the sake of Brandon, who was best friends with his dad and our son getting to know his grandfather, I invited him to move in with us to help him fully recover from his injuries. That night I would address the issues relating to my marriage that I had been quietly grappling with for some time.

I knew passively approaching him and saying, "Hey, I have noticed some peculiar behavior you have been exhibiting," would get me nowhere. So, I decided to go the old school route to find out what my man was doing by simply looking through his phone. This approach wouldn't be complex because I paid the bills and set up all our accounts, so I had his password. I hopped to it with all the necessary information because I could not shake my gut feeling that something was terribly wrong. Ignoring my spirit any longer would be the death of my soul. My heart began beating out of my chest while I thought about the old cliche, seek, and you shall find. I understood what I was about to get myself into. My eyes were wide open, and my heart was down for whatever, or so I thought! I took a deep breath, then turned on the computer that I always left on the nightstand next to my side of the bed.

When I first logged into Brandon's cell phone account, everything looked fine.

There weren't any long conversations, and all calls lasted less than five minutes. I started to feel relieved until I began seeing numbers repeating and a pattern in the times of his outgoing calls. Noticing that I had been holding my breath as I focused on my discovery, I told myself, "Breathe, girl, do not pass out before you find out what you are looking for." Then, I took a huge gasp of air. After getting some much-needed oxygen, I began to relax. At first, I thought my husband had been talking to his coworkers because the calls mainly were made after he left for work. His cell phone service provider highlighted the most frequently called numbers, and that's when shit started popping!

Now I'm noticing as soon as he leaves the house, he calls the same numbers each night. I couldn't believe it! This mother fucker never had anything to say when he was home with me. He was always quiet as a mouse, so I wondered who he was calling and what they were talking about. As I sat on my bed with my mind blown away by what I was looking at, I contemplated whether I should call the numbers to find out exactly who was on the other end of each line.

Even though I wanted to, my inner Superwoman came over me and said, "No, Bitch, you will not call another woman about your husband and look dumb as hell." On top of that, the woman would have my number and could call at will to share all the graphic details of her escapades with my husband. I wasn't about to go out like that. My inner thoughts were sadly pointing to the reality that my husband was having an affair. *Damn*!

In shock, I kept telling myself not to run up the stairs to snatch Brandon's ass, punch him in his throat, and drag him across the floor. Instead, I decided to wait until he came downstairs and casually asked for his phone. Brandon had no reason to question my request because we were not fighting. Plus, in all the years we had been married, I hardly accused him of cheating. With all life's challenges, I did not even have time to allow myself to think that way; adding more distractions was something I could not handle. Flying off the handle before getting to the bottom of this investigation was useless, so I controlled the heat rising in my body and waited for him to come to bed.

When the game ended, I heard my husband walking down the stairs toward our bedroom. Brandon entered the room. Before a second could pass, I blurted out, "Let me see your phone!" While trying to appear cool and collected. He looked at me suspiciously as I held my gaze in such a way that he knew he didn't have a freaking choice. I had already written down the frequently called numbers from his phone bill to dial them whether he gave his phone up or not. I thought, *Were these numbers for his coworkers or women? If they were women, I knew we had a problem because my husband didn't talk to women for sport. If he was talking to a woman, he was fucking her, or he was trying to.* Brandon cautiously handed me his cell phone with a stupid look on his face. Here we go!

With the phone in my hand, I dialed the first number and simultaneously prayed that a man would be on the other end. I wanted my husband to say, "My bad, bro, I dialed your number by mistake." Not so lucky. The first number out the gate led to a woman's voicemail! *Got damnit!* My heart was racing like crazy, but this didn't dissuade me. I dialed the second number. There was no voicemail message, just a machine recording of the number. *Okay, okay, deep breath!*

I dialed the third number, and a woman answered. Bingo! When the mysterious woman said "hello," I punked out and hung up quickly. Was I losing my Superwoman power? I thought, "*Girl, get it together! Now is not the time to lose your courage. Gather your strength and uncover whatever it is that has been stirring in your spirit to settle your suspicions once and for all because it appears that shit is about to go down!*" After taking a minute to gather myself, I stared at the idiot standing in front of me with a you-got-something-to-tell-me face. He says, "I don't know who that was," with a straight face so that he could appear like he was telling the truth.

Right at that moment, our son came into the bedroom and interrupted what could have been a volatile situation. As if nothing was happening, we silently laid him on our bed and got him to sleep before we continued with the number roulette game we'd been playing. I led Brandon to another room toward the back of the house. This time, I put the phone on speaker before dialing the fourth number. Wouldn't you know it? Another woman answered! When she said "hello," I mouth to him to speak. Instead, his stupid ass started telling me he didn't know who the woman on the other line was. I was unconvinced, so I grimaced and pushed the phone to his face, telling him to say something. But he continued to whisper that he didn't know who the woman was.

I couldn't help but laugh a little because this man was lying his face off. Knowing he was lying, I pondered the reality that he was likely having an affair, but I felt like it was something we could handle together. We'd been married for fourteen years and together for twenty-one; this was something we could work through, no problem. After a few minutes, the woman on the phone said, "Hello?" My husband whispered that he didn't know this person.

In an oh-no-you-didn't voice, the woman yelled, "You don't know me, Brandon?"

Oh, this bitch done said his name! Brandon didn't react when the mysterious woman called him out by name. He was sticking to his story that he did not know who the woman was. The only difference was that he had the guiltiest look I'd ever seen on his face; he was starting to shrug his shoulders like a child. I hung up the phone and knew the life I thought I had with Brandon was about to crumble like a boulder falling during an avalanche.

Discovering that the numbers my husband frequently called belonged to other women, not coworkers, led me to second guess my decision to look through his phone. *Should I let the woman answering the phone slide and act like the exchange didn't happen? Should I move forward and get to the bottom of the bullshit that was currently in play?* Finally, I was allowing myself to listen to what God was revealing to me. It was time to do something different, so I let the pain I felt in my heart come forward, listened to my spirit, and followed my gut. These choices were long overdue.

Like I said before, I ignored God when He tried to get my attention prior to this day. The signs of my husband's bullshit were there way before I even thought to look through his phone and confront him. Brandon had been telling on himself through his actions for some time. The most significant sign was that he had not touched me or made any sexual advances since the day I told him I was pregnant. Now, that's some suspicious shit. In addition to this behavior, the other usual red flags were there. He bought new underwear, took showers before and after work, and left early for work every day. I have never known a person who began work at 11 pm and chose to go in at 8 pm. *That's some Bullshit!*

I must admit that Brandon leaving early for work didn't bother me until our son was born. He always made his escape while I was bathing our newborn. He more than likely chose that time because I was focused on our baby's needs and would not allow myself to be distracted and switch my attention to him. One day I asked, "why he was leaving for work so early?" He told me he wanted to have time to relax and prepare for his night. Had I known he meant he needed to go get some pussy before he started his day, I probably would not be telling this story from a cozy space!

Another red flag should have ended our marriage, but I decided to turn a blind eye. The incident happened about nine months after I gave birth to my son. While putting away my husband's laundry, I find an empty erectile dysfunction prescription bottle in his dresser drawer. I thought there was nothing to panic about because he had high blood pressure and may need the pills now and then. However, after looking closely at the pill bottle, I realized the prescription was dated for the same month I had given birth! This was a huge problem because Brandon had not touched me in over a year at this point. I was raging mad.

Honey, I was ready to fight when I found Brandon's pills. I did not wait or brush the bullshit aside. Instead, I confronted him as soon as he got home. Of course, he lied and said he was selling the pills to his coworkers, but I knew better. I knew he was lying, but I also knew how real this situation was because when I hit him. Brandon tried to defend himself from my attack, which let me know he didn't give a damn about how the situation looked or made me feel.

I became even more upset because Brandon always stayed calm whenever I got upset with him. Without hesitating, I immediately told Brandon to move out. He agreed, which he never did during an argument, even if I was acting like a raging banshee woman, screaming and hollering at the top of my lungs. Brandon quickly called a family member to ask if he could stay with them because I was putting him out.

After things settled down, Brandon slept in the guest room that night and went to crash at a family member's house the next day. I was devastated that my marriage seemed to be ending before our son's first birthday. I felt I would be leaving my son at a disadvantage if I agreed to end my marriage so early in his life. I was adamant about giving my son a chance to grow up in a two-parent home, and I needed to figure out how to get past Brandon cheating. So, I reverted to how I was socialized growing up. I carried on as if nothing had happened between us and hid my anger. I swept all my feelings under the rug for the sake of my family.

This night, my eyes were wide open! Once I realized all the numbers dialed belonged to females, who appeared to be familiar with my husband, I knew it was time to see what was unfolding before me. All the lights in the house were off, so it was completely dark. I began my interrogation. If I was going to have a shot at finding out who his mistress was, I had to be calculated and calm. Careful not to use my angry-woman- "this-is-some-bullshit" voice, I switched my tone to sound caring and willing to forgive. To start, I asked about the Girl who said his name when I dialed her number. *Could she be the reason my marriage was slowly disintegrating?* I wanted to find out.

"Who is she?" I calmly asked.

Without hesitation, Brandon replied, "I don't know."

I ask again, and he pauses before opening his mouth to answer.

I knew I had to put pressure on his ass to get him to come out with the truth, so I said, "If you don't tell me exactly who that was, I am going to fuck your ass up!"

So much for the calm, forgiving tone, I wanted to maintain.

My husband knew I had violent tendencies, so he took a deep breath and paused again. I uttered one more threat before offering him a chance for forgiveness because I consider myself a down-to-earth woman who understands men. My father raised my two brothers and me from the age of twelve. I witnessed my father, uncle, and brothers run through women until I was grown. At this time in my life, I believed that a man having an affair was no big deal; couples could work through infidelity if both parties decided to stay together. With this perspective in mind, I asked Brandon for the truth. Brandon swallowed so hard I could hear how dry his mouth was. This mother fucker was nervous as hell! All of this confirmed that something was up because Brandon never cared about shit. *Oh shoot, it's about to get real!*

Usually, I can brace myself for hard conversations and bad news. My instincts told me to keep pressing Brandon, but they also said to sit my super juicy self-down. The atmosphere felt like it was about to explode! You could hear a pin drop because it was so quiet.

I anxiously said, "Mother fucker, you better tell me the truth!" Then, my husband began to speak.

"The guys at the job talk during our lunch breaks about how you can meet any kind of woman you want." It's like he started explaining things in mid-conversation, so I probed him for more information. I asked, "Where do they meet these women?"

"A black book," he replied.

I thought, "*This man is lying his face off.*"

First of all, Brandon is not about to read a book for nothing in the world. Second of all, there aren't any bitches in a black book in the 21st century! "A book?" I asked, remaining calm and focused. "What kind of women?"

Brandon froze.

I screamed, "say it! What is it?"

After what felt like five minutes of awkward silence, Brandon finally opened his mouth and spoke in a barely audible voice. "Escorts."

"I couldn't believe what I'd heard, so I said, "Excuse me? What the fuck did you say?"

"Escorts," he repeated.

"As in bitches you give money too?!" I screamed in astonishment.

After a few seconds of silence, I spoke up. "You have got to be kidding me!"

I spent the entire night waiting for Brandon to admit to having an affair with one woman, who probably would've become my nemesis or some shit. Never in my wildest dreams did I expect my husband of fourteen years to tell me that he was cheating with a plethora of females he had been hitting up in their DM's! Yes, there was a black book; it was called social media! Before that night, I did not know this big ass fool knew how to search for anything on the damn Internet, but I learned that night that he knew how to find himself some pussy. Brandon's confession left me flabbergasted and uncharacteristically speechless! Who I thought I was as a wife changed forever in the darkness of our living room. I could not process the fact that my husband was trolling the social media streets being a hoe and letting all kinds of females tell him just enough to get his money. He was dumb as fuck.

My mind raced with thoughts of where Brandon and I were in our marriage as new parents. My hopes for my child's future were at risk. It was important for my son to love the Lord, learn to speak foreign languages, play musical instruments, excel at sports, and become academically strong. I wanted him to know he is loved, be happy, and live prosperously. I wanted my child to have the confidence to rule the world and come from a two-parent home. Instead, in one night, my dreams for my son were altered.

I began to doubt if those things could happen in my son's life, especially since I was contemplating murdering his father. I wondered, *Were Brandon and I about to shatter the family foundation I thought we were building? Could I forgive Brandon for the sake of our family unit? Was I willing to sacrifice my feelings and heartbreak to ensure my child had his father in the home?* First, I had to overcome my intense desire to hurt Brandon. This feeling was alarming to my spirit. While we were still in our dark living room, I made the first attempt to sneak attack Brandon's ass and punch him straight in his throat, but it was unsuccessful.

You might've heard marriage horror stories about a husband or wife cheating with another person and, perhaps, having a child outside of the marriage. For me, this would be hurtful, but it is something couples can get past. People face horrendous betrayals by their partners every day, and marriage vows are broken for various reasons. What was I supposed to do with Brandon's admission to having multiple affairs? How could I wrap my brain around my husband having sex with Internet hoes for the last three years of our marriage? Why would he wait until I was pregnant with our first child to act like an idiot? Had he been doing this throughout our entire marriage? If I had any hope of raising BJ, my son, in a healthy environment, I needed to get to the bottom of things and find out how his father and I got to this point.

I know countless women who live the rest of their lives wondering what was wrong with them. How could I avoid becoming them? What did I need to do to not carry the shame of my husband cheating in such a reprehensible way? First, I needed to discover the pathology of these continuous occurrences. It was imperative to find out what led my husband to this level of betrayal and disrespect toward me. What made Brandon think for a second that he could get away with such salacious behavior? Something had to be missing in my life that I could stand so close to such despicable deception without blinking and allow it to go on for three years? We both had to be in pain from experiences so severely traumatic that we chose to suffer in silence rather than trust each other enough to share our troubles.

Although I made the common mistake of not trusting and ignoring my gut feelings about Brandon, I had to push through and determine what this behavior was a manifestation of. Compelled to uncover why I was complicit in my heart's wrongdoing; it was imperative to conjure up the emotional strength and courage to discover my role in accepting mistreatment from others. My pain and desire to be completely present for my son brought me to a place of willingness to understand what I know now as the trauma I experienced growing up. It was time to take responsibility for my unhappiness and do the work of self-discovery. It was time to dig deep, open the wounds of my soul, and begin my healing journey to become an incredible mother and woman who lived entirely in love and joy.

CHRONICLE II
MY FAKE ASS MARRIAGE

I was strong and intelligent. I didn't take any shit from men. I was an educated professional. I built my own home. I was married for twelve years to the same man before I became a mother. I thought I was doing everything right and in order, as church people say. I took my time. We stayed together for so long. How could this happen to me? How could this happen to so many women like me? Did I miss something, or did I refuse to see my husband's betrayal for what it was?

The following day after my investigative confrontation, several revelations of how fake my marriage was and how my idea of love was displaced most of my life came. I could not help but wonder if love was a lie. How did I get here? I thought I was doing everything right. I woke up to the phone ringing off the hook. My godmother was calling, so I automatically assumed she wanted to check on my son. As I began to tell her what happened, to my surprise, she already knew what went down because my stupid ass husband had already told her. As a matter of fact, he called just about everyone, including my parents and brothers, to tell them what he had done! *You have got to be kidding me!* Not only did this mother fucker not give me time to process what happened, but he also single-handedly humiliated me in front of everyone I cared about. This bitch ass was trying to gain sympathy from my family before I had a chance to talk to anyone. Why couldn't he call his family and tell them he was fucking hoes?

The night after Brandon's confession, I sent BJ to his grandmother's house for the weekend knowing I needed to have a conversation with my husband without worrying if he would wake up and hear our conversation like he did the night before. BJ watched us talking in the living room and ran back into the bedroom while crying uncontrollably. He did not want either of us to pick him up, as if he intuitively knew something was seriously wrong between his parents. For this reason, I had to handle the situation as conscientiously as possible because it was apparent how aware my son was at two years old.

I waited for Brandon to return from work. Once he did, I wanted us to have a calm conversation about everything. My father-in-law was upstairs in his room, so I planned to keep my cool. We settled into the evening as if my world had not shattered the night before. Brandon sat on the loveseat in the master bedroom, and I sat on our king-sized bed. Acting like I could not remember what he shared the night before, I began my second round of interrogations.

"Now, who did you say you were fucking?"

"Where did you find these women again?"

"Why did you say you wanted to do this?" I waited for Brandon's answers.

He said, "It was something I always wanted to do."

Just like that!

Honestly, discovering that this bastard wanted to sexually engage with escorts took something out of me.

My soul felt like it was in a heavyweight boxing match, and I was losing the title fight. *Did he just tell his wife that he always wanted to fuck escorts?* This man had not touched me since the day I told him I was pregnant. As a married woman, I had not been touched by my husband or any other man in three years. Now, what in the hookah whookah was going on with me!

I slept next to Brandon every night. When I was pregnant, I begged him to have sex with me, but he never would. I was so horny while pregnant, but I didn't push the issue because he told me that he didn't want anything to happen to the baby because I had a high-risk pregnancy. After giving birth, I began to raise my eyebrow, knowing something was up but chose to ignore it! Although my husband had not touched me, I remained faithful the entire time. I worked in a male-dominated industry and still did not talk to anyone else or flirt.

Focused on being a new mother, a good wife, and a responsible caretaker to my father-in-law was enough to fill my plate. The strangest thing about Brandon's demeanor during the second interrogation was that it seemed he had no remorse or regret about what he was doing. He was so sure of himself. He thought it was proper also to admit that he was no longer sexually attracted to me once I told him I was pregnant. *Son of a bitch, you feeling yourself like that?!*

Brandon wounded my ego for sure, and his inability to empathize pissed me off even more. On that day, I promised myself that he would pay for being so careless with my heart. I began to stare at him and quietly ponder my next move. How would I show him that he could not make me feel ashamed or less worthy of affection? After thinking it over, I felt the need to prove myself as a sexually desirable woman. In retaliation, I quickly jumped off our bed, entered my walk-in closet, and put on my raunchiest peach lace lingerie. It was something a man addicted to hoes would not look twice at, so to ensure insult, I also pulled out all the vibrators and dildos I owned! Re-entering the bedroom, I saw a look of confusion on Brandon's face.

I was about to prove to this deceitful man that I was desirable, sexy, and still had it as a woman! Who the heck did this less than mediocre dick man think he was?! He was about to find out whose soul he was relentlessly trampling over. I climbed on our big ass bed, crawled to the middle, and began to play with the pussycat. I started pleasuring myself in such a dramatic animated way that I knew would turn him on. I had his full attention now. Since he frequently watched porn, I became a porn star. The corny moaning noises girls make in those flicks, I made them.

For a quick second, I remembered his father was upstairs and hesitated, but I decided to say, fuck it! *Let him hear this shit, too.* I got loud, very loud. I went from my fingers to my vibrator. While pleasuring myself, this fool thought I wanted him to join me. He hadn't touched me in three years and just told me he wasn't sexually attracted to me, but he had the nerve to get off the couch and walk to the bed like he was supposed to be part of me finally getting my rocks off.

Entrenched in what I was doing, Brandon got on his knees and reached for me. Again, the man who didn't want me anymore was suddenly trying to pull off my panties! When he reached for me, I kicked him and told him to get off me because he was fucking up my nut! Confused, Brandon stopped and began to watch more intently.

Then I picked up my big black dildo, probably ten times the size of Brandon's dick, and began to pleasure myself with it and the vibrator simultaneously.

Confused, he said, "What can I do?"

I got mad and happy all at the same time. I was mad because I hadn't done this a long time ago when I first suspected something was off with my husband and happy, I was doing it in front of him. After all, that shit felt so good. I was experiencing a level of ecstasy I had not felt in a long time. At first, I was loud because I wanted to be vindictive, but I quickly grew louder because I was about to release an orgasm that had been pinned up for three long years! Have mercy! My body was exploding, and it felt fantastic.

After the much-needed explosion, I cleaned up, got dressed, and began asking "why" questions. The best way to understand any situation is to ask "why" because it eliminates confusion caused by assumptions fueled by a lack of information. Usually, people want to identify who's at fault or who caused the betrayal, wanting to know if they are ultimately the reason for the act. Brandon's "why" was because he fucking felt like it and was hoping he wasn't going to get caught. Why else would he do something that he absolutely knew was going to hurt his wife, the mother of his child? It was painful to hear that my husband was no longer attracted to me. It was humiliating, and it shook me in such a way that I knew it was time to address the mistreatment and betrayal head-on.

I refused to act like a woman with an "S" on her chest and continue in our marriage like this man didn't just stomp the blood from my heart. Sitting on my bed, I stared quietly at Brandon as he calmly sat back down on the purple couch in our bedroom.

The sight of him brought a wave of anger that overtook my body. In a daze, I got up to lock the door and could sense Brandon's father on the other side. He must have known before me that I was getting ready to murder his son.

Before losing control, I had the forethought to make sure I protected myself against anyone coming in to attempt to save my husband. With the door locked, I began to scream the questions I already knew the answers to. Not knowing how the wire hangers got in my hand, I suddenly started lashing him with them. I grimaced and shouted. If he tried to hit me back, I would kill him. How dare he do this and destroy our family for some pussy! When the hangers were not doing what I needed them to do, I jumped on his lap and began punching him with my fists, choking and scratching him in a rhythm that felt primal. Beyond enraged, all the emotions I had been suppressing over the years came flooding into the room. I blacked out.

Intuitively, I knew I was in the midst of killing my husband, then in an instant, I stopped. A stillness came over me. It was like God was saying to me, "No, don't do it." Listening to my spirit, I looked at Brandon and knew everything I thought was love was untrue. I had an epiphany that revealed Brandon and my marriage were fake. With all that transpired that night, I knew that my heart, soul, and everything I thought was love had been an utter lie.

Blessed to experience the feeling of true love since becoming a mother allowed me to measure what was missing in my marriage. I could unpack the feelings I did not understand when Brandon did not go the extra mile for me. Unguarding my heart for my child's love exposed the love that my husband and I said we had for each other was fake.

The absence of love for Brandon started an ache in my soul that I could no longer ignore. I instinctively felt divorce was inevitable. However, I had not yet connected the dots. Something wasn't right; I wasn't ready to accept or see what was going wrong in my life, especially the issues in my marriage. Being with Brandon that night, doing the things I did to release my anger and pain, revealed my reality that I was going through life by numbing all the hurt of a loveless marriage with other things, especially cake.

Every emotion began running through my body. As I stood there, I felt the numbness from our fourteen-year marriage disappearing from my body. The cold steel of my hardened heart was filling up with warm, uncontrollable pain that moved around my body like an electric blanket. I was unable to do anything to soothe the enormous pain I had been swallowing for most of my life. The severity of pain coming from my heart was alarming. I opened my eyes to make sure it was still inside my chest. The ache in my soul began to wash the naivety away. Conscious of grasping the truth that the man who sat in front of me was not the man I vowed to have and hold for the rest of my life. He had been hiding his true self from me for over twenty years.

I had to take a step back and look within myself to get to the bottom of the "why." Clearly, I buried my pain, and my husband hid his deceitful behavior and unwillingness to be honest about wanting to be with other women. If you find yourself in a similar situation, it is crucial to allow people to be their authentic selves no matter what. If you don't, it will force them to conform to who they think you want them to be when they are in front of you, not who they really are when you are not present.

Essentially people begin hiding instead of having the courage to be their true selves good, bad, or indifferent. Blind to Brandon's authentic self, I subsequently gave him too many passes based on who I thought he was.

My pain prevented real love from entering my heart until my son was born. I needed to uncover how I agreed to become Brandon's wife in such a broken state? At times, my pain was tremendous and unbearable. I prayed to God for the courage and strength to become healed enough to forgive those I had unknowingly permitted to damage my heart. I was ready to live life differently by taking charge of the love I deserved. It was time to stop accepting the subpar behavior people were giving me. It was time for mother fuckers to level up!

CHRONICLE III
THE BROKENNESS WAS NECESSARY

When I had my son, a light came into my heart, and it was as bright and warm as the sun. I wanted to do my best for him. Hearing Brandon's truth was the catalyst to begin a journey that would save me from a lifetime of bitterness, shame, humiliation, and a sense of unworthiness. I opened my spirit to receive God's revelation that the enemy wanted to destroy me and was trying to do so through the destruction of my family.

Taking steps to overcome my hurt, I used this revelation as armor to protect my own heart and commanded the enemy to flee from my life! I was determined to do whatever it took to keep my family safe and intact. The first part of my healing journey began with discovering why I had experienced so much betrayal and mistrust when it came to love. Why was I so broken?

When I was eighteen years old, I graduated from high school. My mother, whom I had not lived with since I was twelve, came to town from New York for my graduation. I remember how proud and joyful she was that day. She had so much hope for my future and prayed for my success. She was a newly ordained minister and had taken her place as an assistant pastor of a church.

The night before my graduation ceremony, my mother made it a point to tell me that she loved me and emphasized the love God had for me. She explained love from a biblical perspective as we sat in the middle of her bed in her hotel room and read 1 Corinthians 13 aloud. As I reflected on that night, I know now that my mother wanted me to understand the importance of love before I embarked on a new phase in my life. I didn't understand it then, but I recognize now what she was giving me.

Before my high school graduation, the enemy's trick began to set the stage in my life. As a vibrant teenager, I didn't recognize the attacks against my life as the enemy attempting to beat me down. He tried to make sure my spirit was so broken that, once he pounced on my soul, he would annihilate me and keep me from living a life of love and prosperity. The blatant attacks to break my spirit started when my father remarried (she will be the wife without a name).

On the day this woman moved into the home I shared with my brothers and father, she cornered me inside the back bedroom while my father was outside unloading her things. She was eager to show me a letter my mother had written asking her to help me become a young woman since she would be the woman of the house. It made perfect sense to me. However, this woman said cunningly that my mother asked her to take me shopping, show me how to dress like a lady, teach me how to wear make-up properly, etc. While talking to me, she looked out the window to make sure my father was still outside. Then, she said, "Don't ask me for shit." I'm not doing anything for you or your brothers. "I married your father, not the three of you. And do not forget it." I was shocked and caught off guard! I thought *This bitch was phony as hell!*

Before the wedding, she presented herself as caring and wanting to be a part of our family. When she and my father were dating, I liked her conniving ass! Thinking back on it, I should've paid closer attention when I walked into her bridal room the morning of the wedding, excited to see her dress. The dramatic heifer started screaming and trying to hide under the bed. She covered her face and cried, "Don't let her see me! Don't let her see me!"

I thought, *what in the world is wrong with her? Did I do something wrong?*

Shit, I was sixteen, but I knew it was the groom who wasn't supposed to see the bride before the wedding, not his daughter. This woman was supposed to be my new stepmother. I had not lived with a mother figure since I was a young girl, so I would finally have another woman in the house. Being pushed out of the bridal room by the other women made me feel embarrassed and unwanted. The sense of rejection I felt was overwhelming. Her actions should have been a warning sign, and I was clueless about what I would endure later.

Going back to the morning of graduation, I remember that my mother woke me excited about the promise of our future. I had to go to my graduation rehearsal that afternoon which was down the street from the hotel. I thought to myself, *Why didn't I bring a change of clothes?* In my spirit, I knew it wasn't a good idea to go home, but I had to shower and change my clothes.

When I arrived home, I immediately called my cousin Bridgit to ask her to give me five dollars to pay off my school balance and get my diploma. After sharing one of the most moving experiences, I'd ever had with my mother the night before, I could not do anything to disappoint her. She was so proud of me.

While I was on the phone with my cousin, the other line rang. It was a call for the wife.

Her pharmacist friend was on the line. I knew I wasn't supposed to tell an adult to call back if they were calling for my father or his wife, but I had to finish talking to my cousin to make sure she gave me the money to get my diploma! I told the wife's friend she could call back, or I would tell the wife to call her in five minutes. In my haste, I forgot to tell the wife to call her friend. *Lord, why did I make that mistake?* The enemy was about to gain ground, and the trajectory of my life was about to go way off course.

The pharmacist friend called back five minutes later, but that wasn't good enough. Because I didn't give the wife the phone when her friend first called, she came downstairs and knocked on my bedroom door. I was sitting at my pampering table and curling my hair when the wife entered and said how disappointed she was about me not giving her the phone.

By my senior year of high school, I despised this woman. Holding on to my mother's positive words over my life the night before, I decided not to let her make me angry. It was best to be nice and go along with what was happening at that moment. Disregarding that this was supposed to be my day of celebration, she began saying that no one in my family cared about me. Only people from her family sent me graduation cards and money.

She was lying, and I was determined to keep going and not let her words affect my mood for the day. I let her speak and did not say a word. After gathering myself, I proceeded to leave and catch the bus to go to my graduation rehearsal.

After rehearsal, my classmate, Charles, asked if he could come home with me to change his clothes and ride with me to our graduation. I agreed. Charles and I hopped on MARTA to head back to my house. Our lives were full of hope and aspiration; we were ready to conquer the world. That day was the best day ever. What could go wrong?

When Charles and I got to the house, another friend called to ask if my dad could pick her up for the ceremony because it was too hot for her to catch the bus. In a typical family situation, this would probably not be a problem. However, all my close friends knew that my father did not do any extras for me. He rarely dropped me off or picked me up from anywhere, regardless of the distance. I almost always had to figure things out on my own if I needed to go anywhere or do anything significant. With this said, my girlfriend knew dang well my father wasn't going to pick her up. After I firmly reiterated this fact to her, she pleaded for me to ask him anyway because he might agree since it was my graduation day. I felt remarkable about my accomplishment, so I allowed my friend to persuade me to ask my father to pick her up.

My father came home while she and I were still on the phone. When he walked into the kitchen, I told my friend to hold on. I took a deep breath and stuttered a little before asking him for this favor. As expected, my father refused. He said his best friend and the friend's girlfriend were riding with him to the ceremony. Immediately, as if on cue, he started fussing as usual about me not asking him for anything. I couldn't believe it. It was my day! He was supposed to be happy and proud of me like my mother was.

I didn't realize I had been standing in front of him with my mouth wide open and my hand on my hip while the other hand still held the phone. That was a position of disrespect, and the enemy used the exchange between my father and me to break me! Without warning, my father slapped my hand off my hip like it was a regular Friday afternoon. No big deal.

As I stood there, still holding the phone and completely mortified, he continued to slap my hand while telling me that I was disrespectful for asking him for a favor. He also brought up that I had not given his wife the phone earlier that morning when her friend called. While he was slapping and yelling, I saw his wife enter the kitchen from my peripheral view. When she saw what was going on, she turned around slowly and returned to wherever she came from. Then, my father uttered something that I'll never forget.

My father adjusted his aim, looked me straight in my face, and said, "You are not graduating today; I am. You didn't do the twelve years; I did." After slapping me in my face several more times, he asked if I was mad because he was tired of seeing my crocodile tears. Was I mad? I was devastated! How could my father, of all people, hit and yell at me on my graduation day?! We were supposed to be celebrating. I was the first of his three children to graduate from high school. I was the second oldest but graduated before my eldest brother because he got kicked out of school for dating the principal's daughter.

On my special day, I thought he would be pleased with me for a change and show me love, as my mother did. Unfortunately, this wasn't the case; I mustered the courage to respond to his question and said, "If this is your graduation, you should go ... I'm not going." Storming to my room, I cried uncontrollably and felt horrified by the fact that Charles witnessed the entire fiasco unfold. I vowed that I was not going to the graduation. In this moment of sorrow, my baby brother came into my room to console me. He told me to go to graduation anyway, then wiped my tears and did his best to help me put on my make-up. He reminded me that I had company. We needed to be getting on our way, so we did.

Charles and I walked in silence. We acted as if nothing happened, the typical cover-up. Out of respect, I yelled upstairs to tell my father that I was leaving. Silently, I wondered how much of the incident my friend on the phone had heard. Although I felt highly embarrassed and ashamed, I looked forward to seeing her and our other friends at the graduation ceremony. It turned out that my ass whopping was in vain because she and another friend didn't even show up to my graduation.

Marching into the Civic Center auditorium with my class, I saw my mother practically in the middle of the aisle. She was elated and could not contain her joy. As I watched her take tons of pictures, I did my best to hold back tears. I did not want her to see how broken I had become in the short time since she last saw me. As soon as I walked past her, the warm crocodile tears began rolling down my face. This cry was ugly. I couldn't tell you who I sat next to during the ceremony because I wept so hard and literally could not see past my tears.

After the ceremony, I went back to the designated room to get my diploma cover. On my way, I saw my father, the wife, my father's friend, and the man's girlfriend. They were laughing, joking, and having a good time. Then, my father had the nerve to lean toward me to congratulate me. My body stiffened. How dare he act like he did not destroy my spirit! Despite this, I mumbled "thank you" while his friend looked at us. Although I was hurt, I hoped that he would try to redeem himself and give me a gift or take the family out to celebrate.

Without fail, he chose to leave the ceremony with his wife and friends. Unphased, I found my mother standing outside the Civic Center and asked her if she wanted to go to dinner. She hugged me and said she was going back to her room to get some rest. Not wanting to hurt her, I didn't mention what happened with my father. I decided to go to dinner with my cousin and her family. When I returned home that night, I went upstairs as I usually did to tell my father I was in the house. Secretly, I wanted him to apologize for mistreating me earlier, but I got nothing.

As I prepared to go to bed, I began reflecting on the Bible verses my mother had read to me the night before. Within twenty-four hours, the enemy succeeded in convincing me that I did not deserve to be loved or wanted. There must have been a mistake. The words of the Apostle Paul in 1 Corinthians 13 had to be an error, a joke.

That night, I lost sight of the masterpiece God was creating in me because of my father's thoughtless mistreatment. The enemy tricked me into believing that no other man could love me since my father acted like he did not. My father's careless act broke me so severely; I carried the pain in a way that changed how I thought others should treat me. My confidence had disappeared way before my husband's confession.

Instead of trusting my mother, believing the Bible, and all that God had for me, I allowed the enemy to usher in an extreme sense of unworthiness to come upon me. Using the man who raised me as a vessel to destroy my hope for love and accomplishing my dreams, a downward spiral ensued with no chance of catching my balance. That night, I officially became a lost soul.

CHRONICLE IV
TALES OF THE THREE TORNADOES

After reflecting on my formative relationship experiences as a teen and young woman during my healing process, it was time to own that the sterile relationship with my father played a prominent role in how cut and dry I behaved with people when they disappointed me. Why did I tolerate poor behavior from others? I let too many people slide.

I was the only girl when my brothers and I moved to Atlanta with my father before my seventh-grade year of middle school. My brothers and I were very close and did most things together. It was like I was the third son. I was the sibling who checked everyone, fussed, yelled, and fought both of my brothers for any reason. We fought over whose Saturday it was to pick the cartoons we watched and what chores we had that day using buckets and scrub brushes. There were no mops allowed in my father's house.

For my thirteenth birthday, I got my own phone line in my room, which is equivalent to getting a cell phone today. Once that happened, my friends were in my room all the time, calling wrong numbers and meeting boys. The latter was a new concept because I regularly hung out with my brothers and their friends. When my family moved to a new house after my freshman year of high school, my brothers and I had to share a phone. Honey, we would have knock-down, drag-out fights. It was all or nothing when it came to my eldest brother or me using the phone first.

Because my brothers were so big and strong for their age, and I fought with them my entire life, I was not afraid to fight or cuss out anyone who came across my path. My father always tried to get me to temper my attitude for that reason, and probably why I never really argued or fought with my girlfriends. It would have been an unfair fight if I had. I can go from zero to one hundred in seconds, which is not good when developing friendships.

Growing up, I always had guy friends because I was comfortable around boys due to my close relationship with my brothers. I had my first real boyfriend when I was in high school. We will call him "tornado number one" or ("T1") for short. I categorize the three boyfriends I dated in my high school and college years as tornadoes because all their names began with the letter "T," and they helped shaped how I saw myself in relationships until the night of my husband's confession. Tornadoes are classified as weak, strong, or violent. I can honestly say the three men I dated fell into those categories. We'll say T1 was a weak tornado, and T2 was strong. As far as T3, he was violent. Truthfully speaking, he was a fucking EF5 tornado with wind speeds over 200 miles per hour!

I met T1 at a party the night before my fifteenth birthday. He was cool, but we didn't do a lot except talk on the phone. We didn't even go to the movies together. When he came to my house, he always tried to have sex with me. My eldest brother wasn't having any of that, so he banged the door in every time T1 tried anything funny. As time went on, I eventually lost my virginity to T1.

When T1 invited me to his junior prom, my father took me dress shopping. Neither my father nor I knew what we were doing, so we figured it out as we went. My father also let me get my hair done for the dance. Since my mother lived in New York, I learned how to do these girly tasks on my own.

My friends always talked about how ugly T1 was. My mother thought he was ugly too and advised me to pay attention to how the guys I dated looked because I didn't want ugly children. When I got our prom pictures, my girlfriends ripped them apart. They talked about how ugly T1 was, laughed at my shoes, and made fun of my dress. They could not laugh at my hair because it was always thick and a nice length; none of them could say the same about theirs. Instead of snapping back with brutal force because no one invited any of my girlfriends to prom, I only slightly defended myself. Basically, I gave them a pass, and accepted the mistreatment from my so-called girlfriends, and kept it moving.

When I turned sixteen, my father and his wife held a sweet sixteen dinner and invited a few of my closest friends. At that time, I only had two. At dinner, we talked about me working at Six Flags for the summer and T1's senior prom, which he had invited me too again. The stakes were high for this prom because T1 attended the city's most popular new high school; it was a big deal to go to their first prom.

When I told my girls about going to T1's senior prom, we started laughing. I told them I wasn't sure I even wanted to go with him because I didn't like him anymore. Before I could say anything else, my girlfriend, Denise, jumped in and said, "If you don't want to go, I will go with him." I didn't think she was serious, but she followed up by saying, "Ask T1 if I can go with him."

Instead of cursing her stupid ass out, my crazy ass agreed. Adding insult to injury, when I asked T1 if he would go to prom with Denise, his trifling ass said he would go with her! My ass really brokered my first boyfriend and best friend to go to his senior prom together. What was wrong with me?

I was mad as hell about the situation between T1 and Denise, but I did not say a word. Instead, I let it happen. Shit, I made it happen. Now, here is the double-dip. They went to T1's prom together. The plan was for them to stop by Six Flags for Senior Night after the prom. Well, these mother fuckers decided to go to the Senior Night at Six Flags the weekend after T1's prom.

When they got to the park, they stopped by my workstation to greet me and went off to the concert area. On break, I made my way to the concert area and ran right into them. They were standing all out in the open with T1 standing behind Denise; arms wrapped tight around each other like they'd been dating for almost two years. *Well, I'll be damn!* Instead of confronting them, I walked away and returned to my workstation, convincing myself he could have her if he wanted her. I didn't want to admit that I was heartbroken. T1 and Denise going to the prom together was my first traumatic experience involving romantic love.

Despite her betrayal, I continued my friendship with Denise. Accepting and living with feelings of unworthiness, which I experienced in my home, began to manifest in my friendships. Although I didn't know what to call it, I passively co-signed this mistreatment. My eldest brother, while he still lived at home, hung out with college girls.

All the men in my family are considered to be extremely handsome and have no problem with dating anybody they want. When I began hanging out with my eldest brother, who is only fifteen months older than me, he started taking me to the all-girls college one of his girlfriend's attended whenever they had parties. On one particular night, he took me to a Greek step show at the college. At the step show, my brother left me alone to go hang out with his college girlfriend. There was a party in the gym after the step show, so I was fine being by myself. Of course, a nice guy who attended one of the co-ed schools in the University Center asked me to dance. Even though I was a little super juicy, I did pretty well when meeting guys.

Everything about that night was perfect! At least, that's what I thought. In the middle of enjoying myself with the new guy, I looked up and saw T1 across the room! Mind you; I hadn't seen or spoken to him since I witnessed him intimately embracing Denise at Six Flags. He attended the prestigious all-male school in the same University Center, so he stopped by the party to see what was up. Instead of scooping up a nice little college girl, what does he do? He approached me and asked me to dance with him. And my dumb ass agreed.

I was having fun with the nice college guy I'd met at the party earlier, so I should have told T1 to kiss my ass. But noooo! I danced with him and let him kiss me and whisper sweet nothings in my ear. When the party was over, T1 walked me outside. There was a rainy mist in the air, so he waited with me until my brother finally showed up. After that night, I started messing with T1 again, and it ended horribly.

I met T2 while I was working at Six Flags during my junior year of high school. With my father remarried to the crazy lady, I did everything to be out of the house. Now I am completely crushing on T2. So many high school and college students worked at Six Flags that I became friends with people from schools all over Georgia. Although my commute took two hours each way, I always caught the bus to work. It'd drop me off at the front of the park, and I'd walk to the employee section to change into my food service uniform. At the time, I was a Cherry Berry Girl and worked the ice cream stand outside of the dolphin show. T2 worked the grounds, so he was always there in the morning when I walked through the park. I watched him all the time without saying a word.

As time went on, T2 started saying hello, and I shyly greeted him back. We began talking, and it turned out that he was a lot of fun and very silly. Whenever my friends and I went to parties after work, he was always there. If he was talking to another girl, he would leave that girl and come over to talk to me when he saw me. I would say, "Go back to where you came from. Go back and talk to the girl you were talking to." He would reply, "I want to talk to you." Then, we both chuckled and hung out. There was something about us that was cool and comfortable. I felt safe around T2. I don't know if he ever became my official boyfriend, but we hung out a lot. After work, we went to the movies and parties.

Things were pretty rough at home during my junior year. My father's wife was in full effect, acting like a complete idiot. My father told my brothers and me that we had to buy our essential products out of nowhere! I had to buy my feminine items, toilet paper, toothpaste, laundry detergent, etc. His wife insisted that we could no longer make long-distance calls to New York to talk to our mother because she paid the phone bill. She also began locking the freezer whenever she left for work for several days. Since my home life was a mess, I did anything not to go home.

After a while, I found out T2 started going out with one of my classmates, so I stopped hanging out with him to avoid a confrontation. I continued to go to the

University Center with my brother and eventually started attending parties at the all-male college with Denise. Yes, we were still friends even after all the drama with T1. I know. While we were at a party on campus, I met T3, the violent tornado. We danced all night, and I had a ball. Dancing all night might have been nothing to him, but it was everything to me.

Dancing is a way to my heart. I became utterly fascinated with T3 from the moment I met him. I showed up to his dorm room and behaved like a complete bug-a-boo! I was determined to make him my boyfriend. T3 was my type: tall, dark, and kind of handsome. He played basketball for his college team, so I thought he was everything. *What was I thinking?!* I felt so unloved at home; I would have loved a tree if I thought it loved me back!

My eldest brother moved out of the house in his senior year of high school because he hated my father's wife. My youngest brother was in middle school, so we lived in two different worlds at the time. My home was not a home anymore; I spent a lot of time with T3 or my girlfriends and their families. There was so much dysfunction going on with my father and his wife. I must have been looking for a sense of connection, and T3 was my target. Or was I the enemy's target?

Growing up around my brothers and father, I was accustomed to being around men. It was more comfortable than being around girls. Being the only girl in the house worked to my benefit with men because I knew how to fit in. When I wanted something, I usually got it because I had a competitive nature. When I didn't get my way with my brothers, I fought their asses. I had to teach myself not to do this with the men I dated.

As a young teen, my father chipped away at my confidence by speaking negatively into my spirit. He told me he wished he could tear my lips off when I spoke up for myself. He said I was ungrateful and inconsiderate if I asked for something I wanted. Sometimes, the things he said to me were senseless. I had a crush on a player from the San Francisco 49ers who had an unusual name. One Saturday, I was in the living room watching a show called *"Superstars" when* my crush was up to compete. I sat on the couch watching the show in peace, rooting for him, smiling, and cheering. My fantasy boo was winning. I was elated.

My father passed through the living room and looked at the television to see what brought me so much joy. He asked, "What are you watching?" I told him. At some point, I must have mentioned that I liked the football player. Then, my father looked at me in all of my excitement and said, "Well, maybe someone like him would like you if you lost some weight." I went from having a crush to being crushed. My bubble had burst, and, just like that, my fascination for this beautiful species of a man was over.

My father saw me as overweight, which oddly worked in my favor. Due to his perception of me, he was strict about the types of clothes I wore and how I looked. His instruction taught me how to present myself to other males. Because of my father's recommendations, I took pride in how I dressed, even when super juicy girls had limited fashion options at that time.

On the other side of this coin, my father's verbal attacks made me a prime target for T3's attacks. Since I didn't want to go home after school, Denise and I often hung out at T3's dorm with his roommate and other guys who lived on the floor. We played stupid college games like poker and truth or dare? T3 was as broken as I was, but neither of us understood it. We argued and got into fistfights, then made up like nothing ever happened. It was insane. One fall night, I got ready to leave the house to go to T3's dorm as I usually did. When I was about to leave, the doorbell rang. I went to the door, not expecting anyone, and opened it thinking it was one of my little brother's friends. To my surprise, it was T2! We were both silent as we stood in the doorway.

He asked, "How are you doing?"

I replied, "I'm fine," and stepped out onto the porch with him. We lived in a Victorian-style home that had a porch the length of the entire front of the house.

After some more silence, T2 said, "Are you getting ready to go somewhere?"

I answered, "Yes, I'm going to see my friend."

He looked at me and asked, "Who? The guy you were with at the party?"

I immediately responded, "Yes."

After hearing my answer, T2 began sincerely sharing that he didn't want me to be with T3. He said he did not think T3 was a good person for me. I tried to convince T2 that T3 was a nice guy and assured him that everything would be okay. He stood in front of me, wearing his heart on his sleeve. He had on a brown suede jacket, black slacks, and black shoes. I'd never seen him dressed so nicely. That night, he came to my house to ask me to be his girlfriend, but I rejected him. Disappointed, he did the gentlemanly thing and asked if I needed a ride to the train station. I agreed. After a quiet ride to the train station, T2 dropped me off. I did not know the enemy set me up for a soul rupture as I continued to date T3.

Autumn quickly turned into winter. I was home one Friday night when the phone rang. It was T2. I was happy to hear from him because I missed him. We hadn't spoken since the night he came to my house to ask me not to see T3 anymore. After we began talking, he asked me to be his girlfriend. I decided to play hard-to-get and asked him what had happened to his girlfriend. He told me he was not with her anymore and wanted me to give him another chance. To entice me even more, T2 said he would take me wherever I wanted to go. He knew I loved to dance. By this time, I had been going to clubs with my eldest brother. When T2 asked if I wanted him to take me to a club, he knew he had me. He also said we could go out to eat, so I agreed to go to Red Lobster.

Deep down, I wanted to believe T2; I knewT3 was not the right person for me. We fought and argued a lot. I was choosing between two evils: home or him. The EF5 tornado named T3 was still in love with his old girlfriend from his hometown, the girl who had broken his heart, so he didn't trust anyone, and it showed. Knowing how awful T3 was to me, I agreed to go out with T2 the Saturday before Christmas break began. I joked that he would probably stand me up because he wasn't serious about us going out, but T2 insisted he was serious. He said he wanted me to be his woman forever. He said he would call on Wednesday to confirm our date, I agreed, and we hung up.

Before Christmas break that year, T3 asked if he could store his things at my house because he had to clear out his dorm room before leaving campus. Surprisingly, my father allowed him and his roommate to do so, and they came by on the Wednesday T2 was supposed to call me to confirm our date. When T3 and his roommate arrived at my house, all I could do was hope T2 didn't call me while they were there. They finished storing their things, talked for a little while, then left to go back to their hometowns for the holidays. Before going to bed, I laughed silently and shook my head because I knew T2 was not going to call. He was not serious about us getting back together.

At school the next day, I sat and ate lunch like I usually did. When I went to throw away my lunch tray, T2's ex-girlfriend walked up to me.

She calmly said, "Hello."

Confused that she was talking to me, I replied, "Hello." I thought, *what does she want?*

She asked, "Did you hear about T2?"

I looked her in her eyes and responded, "What did he do?"

Then, she said two words I never expected to hear, "He died."

What?! He died?! He was supposed to call me last night! We were supposed to be getting back together! As these thoughts raced through my mind, I saw T2's ex looking at me, waiting for a response. I uttered in disbelief, "Died?!" How? "What happened?"

T2's best friend called her the night before to tell her that he had had a heart attack. She told me that he had had a heart attack once before on his graduation night, but he was able to get to the hospital in time for the doctors to save him. This time, he was not so lucky. I was shocked! I did not know what to say or how to act. I was numb, too numb even to cry.

That afternoon, feeling heartbroken, I shared the news of T2's passing with my father, hoping to receive some comforting words. But that was useless. He made some minor remarks, but that was it. Not knowing what to do, I called T2's number, hoping he would answer. The phone rang about twice, then someone answered!

Please, Lord, let this be a cruel joke.

Please, let this be T2 answering his phone as he always did when I called. When I said "hello," I heard a woman's voice on the other end of the phone. I held my breath.

Please, Lord, let me have the wrong number. I asked the woman, "May I speak with T2?"

With heaviness in her voice, the woman said, "He is not here." Hoping she would give me another reason for his absence, I asked, "Where is he?" She told me that T2 was at the funeral home up the street from his house. Not knowing what else to say, I thanked her and hung up. A couple of days after making that phone call and receiving confirmation that T2 had died, his ex-girlfriend approached me again at school to give me information about his wake and funeral. I wanted to go, but I was afraid to go alone. None of my girlfriends offered to go with me, and I did not want to ask anyone for anything. My father succeeded in instilling in me the notion that I was never supposed to lean on others for support, so once again, I suffered in silence.

Instead of attending T2's funeral, I visited my eldest brother at his apartment because our mother was in town to see him for the holidays. I never forgave myself for not attending T2's funeral, but I will never forget the night of his visit to let me know it was okay. I did not know what love was at that time in my life, but I wish I had. T2 was a strong, positive force in my life. I feel the outcome of my love relationships would have been different if he had lived. His passing became another rupture in my soul that made me cling tighter to T3 instead of leaving him alone as I should have.

My desire to belong when I was a teenager led to intense destructive behavior with T3. My father turned his back on me, and my eldest brother moved out of the house in an attempt to save his own life. The new wife started building her new family with my father and little brother, and she made it clear that I was not a part of it. Barely seventeen years old, I had to fend for myself.

I subconsciously knew I wasn't handling my heart with care. That was the reason why I allowed T1 to use me up by seeing him again after he took Denise to the prom and did God only knows what else with her. It was also why, instead of retreating, I ran toward T3 after losing T2.

I allowed T1 and T3 to crumple me up like I was a piece of aluminum foil, possessing nothing precious about me. Also, I knew my so-called friends were mistreating me, but I held on to the hurt instead of addressing it. I chose to remain silent. I did not advocate for myself then, but I encourage everyone to speak up for yourself if you are going through similar situations. Do not allow the mistreatment to continue. It is so important to recognize what the enemy is doing whenever he attempts to destroy your greatness. It can be scary to lose friends. However, when we acknowledge our worth, it is easier to measure the value of others in our lives. If the person chooses not to adjust their unacceptable behavior, it may be better for their season in your life to end.

Allow these stories of people crumpling and reusing me to be the reason you don't let the enemy prey on your life. Unfortunately, I was unaware of what was happening to me. At that time in my life, my relationship with God was not as strong as it is now; I did not read the Bible unless I was at church. As you can see, the enemy began devouring my spirit before the graduation day attack. The enemy took his time, using insincere relationships with my father, the wife, and friends to prepare my miserable journey of feeling empty and unloved. Without this awareness and my parents' protection, I was powerless to overcome his ploy to destroy me.

CHRONICLE V
THE FOIL EFFECT

I am not a licensed counselor, but I was more than curious to discover the pathology behind my behavior of letting people crumple me up like a piece of aluminum foil. What was the root of not having the courage to stand up for myself and allow others to mistreat me? After the confrontation with my husband, I started going to therapy. During our first meeting, the therapist asked me several questions about my relationship with my parents. After each counseling session, more and more dots began to connect as it related to how I viewed myself when in the presence of others. I began to understand that the relationships I had developed with boyfriends were mainly trauma bonds and unhealthy; they were based on the trauma experienced by my parents and could be the reason for my behavior.

One sign of a trauma bond is craving contact with someone who has hurt you. You know the person will cause you more pain, but you continue to seek their love or attention regardless. I constantly craved my parents' attention. Due to this, I held on to other people who did not care about my feelings, which caused me to try to fit into places where I did not belong.

Often, we think trauma is caused by parents who beat or violently abuse their children, leading to extreme measures of emotional, physical, and mental scars. Good parents, however, do not inflict extreme abuse on their children; they provide safe, comfortable homes. Everything was golden if you were raised in that kind of home; the children came out okay. But did they?

I had to come to grips with the fact that my parents' narcissistic behaviors impacted my life negatively that I created trauma bonds with others. If I were to ask my parents how they did in raising me, they would likely say they did their best. When my father decided to move to Atlanta, my mother told me that she wasn't going, which made no sense to me at all. I thought she was blowing off steam. Perhaps she knew her husband had been cheating on her, and she wasn't going to uproot her life and career for a cheating ass man (something that I now understand as a grown woman). Whatever the reason, my father left and moved to Atlanta while my brothers and I remained in New York until he got settled.

My parents decided my brothers would also move to Atlanta while I stayed in New York. They must have bumped their heads because there was no way I would live somewhere without my brothers. Once they made that announcement, I knew I was going to go to Atlanta with them. My mother had no intention of moving, so I made a choice to live with my brothers. My brothers were my safety net; we always protected each other. I knew I would be safe if I was with them.

When we arrived in Atlanta, my baby brother was nine, and my eldest brother was thirteen. Wow! How courageous was my mom to trust my father to that degree and let her three children move to a new state without her! My brothers and I were mostly on our own when we got to Atlanta. Dad worked the evening shift from 3:00 to 11:00 pm and had to be at work before we got home from school. He left notes for each of us to make the situation work, instructing us what to do when we got home. We had to read the two middle columns of The *Wall Street Journal and Time* or *Newsweek*.

After finishing my homework, I usually had to cook, and my poor brothers had to eat my horrible food. My father hated when I put curry powder in the spaghetti sauce, but I thought it was good. I learned to cook by trial and error but believe me; I can cook my ass off now. As we became older, my brothers and I started spending a lot of time with our friends. Socializing without my brothers got tricky for me. Because I could trust my brothers in any situation, I did not know that I needed to be more cautious with other people. Lord have mercy, I had to learn some vital lessons on trust, and I did.

Moving to Georgia was good for me because I liked the apartment complex we moved to. On our first day there, my brothers and I went to the pool up the street from our apartment. We were in the pool when two neighborhood girls started walking toward us. They wanted to know who we were, where we were from, and what school we attended. They were the know-it-alls of the complex for sure. While living in East Point, there was a strong sense of community. Although we did not live with my mother anymore, my brothers and I continued our family bond. My father was always gone for one reason or another. However, my uncle moved in with us to help, making me the only girl living with all males. Being the only girl in my home, I spent a lot of time at my friends' homes.

After three years, we left East Point and moved to a house in Decatur. I remember feeling so disappointed the first time my father took us to the new neighborhood because gentrification was starting in that area. The house was on a quiet street with modest-sized homes, but it had burned down previously. My father was having it rebuilt for us. I thought my father had lost his mind. *What were we doing moving to such a place?*

Once the house was finished being rebuilt, it looked better than before it burned down; it was huge. I know my father was extremely excited about his accomplishment. On moving day, everything was going great. I had met T1 a few months earlier, so he came over to help us carry boxes and furniture into the house. When he left for the day, I went to the kitchen and put some steaks in the oven. I had a bright idea to put them on broil to cook faster, not knowing that heat from gas stoves was different from the electric stove we had at our apartment in East Point.

I left the steaks cooking in the kitchen and called T1. The next thing I knew, the steaks were on fire! In a panic, I told T1 I would call him back, then attempted to put the fire out. I was too late. The flames were shooting out of the range, and the nobs were melting. Before long, the cabinets caught on fire! I didn't know what to do but call on Jesus and ask him not to burn down my father's brand-new house because I knew I would not survive the outcome.

Jesus answered my prayers. The house did not burn down, but the kitchen was a catastrophe. That fire should have indicated how my life was about to take a turn for the worse. I did not know it then, but the safety nets my brothers provided was about to be removed. Although my father showed me some grace and did not kill me for ruining his new oven, he was insensitive to how he treated me at other times. That, coupled with my mother's absence during a crucial time in my life, made me feel lost and alone.

A year or so after moving to the dreadful house, the foil effect came into play. I had a core group of girlfriends I held on to for dear life; Denise was one of them. Please understand, trauma bonds can be formed in romantic and platonic relationships. My foil effect reference illustrates my poor choices to go back to people who are manipulative and have done me dirty. I stayed in trauma bonds because of my feelings of unworthiness due to the disconnection from my parents. I'm convinced I would have escaped my relationship with T3 sooner if I wasn't crumpled up and tossed away by my father and his wife.

I moved out of my father's house six days after my high school graduation. Things didn't work out, so I moved back into his house after a year and resumed my role as a rent-paying tenant (like how I lived while I was in high school). I had only been back for a month or so when my father told me they would be moving. To be exact, he said they would be leaving Georgia, and I was not invited to move with them to his wife's hometown. Astonished by this announcement, I was unprepared. My oldest brother lived in New York at this time, so I did not have him to rely on. My baby brother was all I had left, and they were taking him away from me. This news left me feeling even more unwanted. I wasn't even twenty years old yet, but my life was a struggle because my parents insisted that I did everything on my own because they said so; I was hanging on by a thread.

My father gave orders without guidance or support. He raised me to be independent of him. He was adamant about me not needing a man for anything, and he was the best man to teach me that lesson. I could not depend on him to help me with anything outside of his immediate role as a parent. I was shocked when he agreed to cosign for the apartment on Peachtree Street that I eventually moved into. It was extremely rare for him to help me with important things outside of food and shelter. He more than likely had a guilty conscience about cosigning with his wife to leave my ass in Georgia to navigate my life alone.

The summer after graduation, I did not plan properly to attend college; I enrolled in classes at the local junior college because it was the most affordable option. After telling my mother that my father wasn't helping me pay for my studies, she sent me a check to assist with my first semester classes. After high school, working and living on my own, I struggled to keep my head above water. All my friends had gone off to four-year colleges, and I was the only one at a junior college. But I was proud of myself because I could pay for all my classes and my books (except my accounting book, which was sixty dollars). I couldn't wait until I got paid to purchase the book because the class moved quickly. I could not go to T3 for money because he was a broke student-athlete.

My other option to get the book was to make a dreaded phone call to my father and ask him to lend me the money. When I called, he said he would think about lending me the money and told me to call him back on Friday for his decision. I called again on Friday, and he did agree to lend me the money. I offered to go to the house to pick it up, but he preferred to meet me at my school to give me the sixty bucks. When he arrived on campus, he got out of the car, handed me exactly sixty dollars, told me he would see me later, then got back in the car and drove away. *Damn!* There was no hug or "how are you holding up?" Nope. He just gave me the exact amount of money I needed and left me alone on that campus street corner.

Although I felt unwanted and lost, I instinctively knew I had to keep pushing myself forward, navigating my life without a roadmap. I had finished my first year at the junior college and was preparing for my second year of college at the local state university. I was going to move on with my life. At least, that's what I thought. Excited and proud that I had found my way and was doing things on my own, I was determined not to let anything, or anyone, pull me down. At the new student orientation, I sat close to the front to make sure I could hear what the school's students and staff had to say. When I finally looked around the room, who did I see sitting a few seats away from me? Fucking T1! *This must be my imagination! What was he doing there? I thought he attended T3's all-male college?*

When I saw T1, I panicked. Paralyzed in my seat; I couldn't move or speak. The truth is, T1 probably wasn't paying me any mind, but I responded to the situation from a position of unworthiness. There was negative messaging floating through my head; I did not understand how to fight it. After that day, I saw T1 in the hall between classes a few times. Since I allowed the enemy to use this boy to convince me that I was unworthy of love and respect, I decided never to return to that college campus for the semester and was ultimately expelled from school for not going to class. Each semester, I would attempt to restart classes and never could overcome my internal battles of unworthiness. Once again, I allowed myself to feel like a piece of foil that had been balled up and discarded.

T3 did not make the foil effect any better. He went back to his hometown the summer I moved into my apartment on Peachtree Street and pretty much harassed me the entire time he was gone. I went to work most days and partied most nights. Against my better judgment, I let Denise move in with me when she asked. Once that happened, her family and friends moved in with her. Her aunt was about nine years older than us, and she and her girlfriends hung out with the popular hot boys in Atlanta.

We had a ball with Auntie showing us the ropes and going to all the local clubs, meeting people every night. Things began to get scary when the hot boys started trying to take over my apartment, which I could not allow. I had to stand up to these men and fight for what was mine. Everybody who lived in my apartment did not see anything wrong with these grown-ass men trying to take over my place. Because men raised me, I saw everything wrong with it and did something about it.

As time went on, T3 returned to the city for school and hated my new lifestyle. We fought all the time. I fought him like I was a man. Based on how I behaved with my brothers, I didn't know it was inappropriate to knock the shit out of a man trying to fight me. I was as horrible to T3 as he was to me. Truthfully, we were both toxic and remained connected through the bond of our similar traumas.

T3 and I once had a fight on Peachtree Street that nearly turned deadly. In the middle of our battle, my uncle just so happened to be at the red light where we were. He saw me fist fighting, then got out of his car and pulled a gun on T3! I heard a man's voice say, "Leave her alone!" When I turned around, I saw that it was my uncle. He was ready to blow T3 away! That was nothing but God intervening. There is not that much coincidence in the world. My uncle, who I had not seen or talked to in forever, would be at that stoplight right at that moment. Instead of killing him, we all went upstairs and talked about everything, and my uncle went on his way. You would have thought I would have left that fool alone after that fight. Nope, I stayed and allowed him to ball me up and reuse me. The aluminum foil effect was plaguing my soul.

I eventually lost the apartment downtown because no one paid the rent. I went to court alone to request more time to pay the past due amount. All the people I allowed to live in the apartment did not wake up that morning to go with me. Why would they? My name was the only one on the lease. I stood in front of the judge and asked for more time, given the standard thirty days to come up with the past due six or seven hundred dollars. When I returned home to tell everyone how much we had to come up with to keep the apartment, they all said they didn't have it. Instead, they would move out. I did not speak up for myself and insisted that they give me their share for living in my apartment rent-free.

Against my better judgment, I called my dad, hoping he would rescue me just like he did when he gave me the sixty dollars for my accounting book. He lived in another state and had made a new life with his wife and my youngest brother. After telling him what happened and what the court said, I asked him to lend me the money I needed to keep my apartment. This time, he didn't take time to think about it. He immediately told me he wouldn't give me the money. And just like that, I was homeless.

I walked the streets of Atlanta with a small tote bag and went from couch to couch. Some nights, I snuck in and slept in T3's dorm room. My father's house was still on the market, so I moved the couch from my apartment into one of the empty rooms and slept on it until the Rent-A-Center people found me and took the sofa back for non-payment. I eventually started sleeping at my play sister's house because I had nowhere else to go. Phyllis and her mom, who I call Momma Dee, invited me to stay with them. Momma Dee did not think I should go from house to house as a young woman. Relieved, I agreed because I needed somewhere safe to live.

When I told my father about my new living arrangement, he came into town and showed up at Momma Dee's house and told her that she should not allow me to stay with them because I had to make my way and stand on my own two feet. Thank the Lord that Momma Dee stood up to my father. She told him it was her decision, and I could stay with her as long as I needed to. Thanks to Momma Dee and Phyllis, I was able to gain some stability in my life. After some time, a former coworker came through when she told me I could live in the dorms at the hospital downtown, if I were a health major at the local university. Bet. I re-enrolled in school and applied to live in the dorm. God was on my side because I got back into school and began living there.

Things seemed to be turning around; my life was getting on track. Unfortunately, that did not last long because that was not the case. There was still one problem: T3 was still in the mist. By the time I was back in school, T3 and I were doing everything possible to destroy each other's lives. We were miserable dating each other.

After a few more years of our volatile relationship, I had enough. I left school and went to New York for a few months to visit with my mother to save me from him. My grandma, fed up with my situation, insisted I go back to school, leave T3 alone, and get on with my life. The day I returned to Atlanta, one of the girls from my floor knocked on my door to tell me that T3 was on the phone. *How in the fuck did he know I was back?!* I had only been back for about twelve hours. *What in the world?* Long story short, I was finally able to leave him, but not before being pushed through a plate glass window and held at gunpoint by one of his other girlfriends, who he also used as a piece of foil.

Mentally and spiritually, I lived in a dark place. The armor of God is the only thing that protected me as I aimlessly walked through life trying to keep me together. Real talk, I positioned myself like a piece of foil; I had no clue how to uncrumple the weak object I had become. Believing the lie, I mistook my platinum crown for tin foil!! The strength it took to live through the self-sabotage due to my destructive internal messaging was miraculous. Unable to break through the poverty mentality I developed since leaving home kept me in a constant downward spiral. I was afraid to ask for help and guidance to achieve my dreams to live the life I wanted. Pride comes before the fall, and I did my best to live a facade that I had it all together. The truth was I desperately needed my parents or anyone who cared about my well-being to swaddle me in their arms and say, come here, child, we got you.

CHRONICLE VI
ALLIES AND ANCHORS

When I reached the lowest point in my life, I began to remember the greatness in me when an unexpected anchor entered my life and saved me. Finally, seeing myself, it was easier to comprehend that the people I surrounded myself with did not have my best interest at heart. I was morphing into something that I was not only to fit in with my social circle. I dressed inappropriately when I went to work and underestimated the potential to follow my original dream to become a doctor. No one knew or could tell that I came from accomplished parents based on how I behaved because I lived entirely independently of them.

It was time to grow up and face the fact that I chose to surround myself with those who were not my friends; they were my allies. What is an ally? An ally is a person who you maintain a relationship with only because you need something from each other. You add value to who they are or what they

need. When they get what they want, the
relationship is over. An ally has an ulterior motive or
is in your life for a season. These relationships are
not sustaining. Perhaps if I had understood this
earlier in life, the feeling of betrayal would not have
plagued my heart for so long. Knowing the
difference between an ally and a friend would have
allowed me to place people where they belonged
at *arm's length.*

While in my twenties, I had not learned my
lessons to rid or defend myself against my allies.
Exemplified by how I continued to accept bullshit
from the people I spent time with. One night at a
popular club in Atlanta, I met a guy, JT, who played
a stint in the NFL. We became fast friends and hung
out often, laughing and having fun. At the time, my
roommate and I hosted big pool parties every
summer. JT and his friends always attended,
showing up jumping in the pool with only their
underwear entertaining all who would watch; they
were the life of the party.

An ally who had been sleeping on my couch at
the time rode to the pool party with me. As soon as I
parked, she stopped me from getting out of the car
and said she had something to talk about. I paused
and looked her directly in her eyes, waiting for her to
speak. After a long pause, she said that she liked JT
and was going to start dating him. Instead of cursing

her out, I told her to go ahead. I felt some way about this, but I held it together, which I was a pro at by this point.

While I was enjoying the party, Denise came in and immediately pulled me to the side to say that she needed five thousand dollars for her business and was going to ask JT to lend it to her. Like an idiot, I told her to go ahead. A few days after the party, JT called and said that Denise asked to borrow money from him and wanted to know if he should give it to her. I told him that he could if he wanted to, and he did. JT and I stopped hanging out after that pool party, even though he called a few months later to tell me that he missed me as his friend. I missed his friendship too; he was always charismatic and had so much swag and finesse. A complete joy to be around, but I had enough of my allies interfering with my male friendships and it was time to move on.

Soon after the pool party, I met Brandon. His friend introduced us because he was too shy to approach me. After much reluctance, I called and asked him to pick me up from the train station; one night, I was stranded with no way home. We began dating after that; I thought he was caring and kind. I thought I could make it work with him, so I told my girlfriends that he was off-limits; no one could try to date or have sex with him. After all, my girlfriends thought it was okay to make fun of his looks, which was always weird because I never talked about the men they dated. There were several incidents that I should have told these so-called friends to kick rocks.

Unaware of the shady actions of women, I was unable to place them where they belonged as allies because I was unwilling to accept that these girls had ulterior motives. At least with Brandon, this is where the buck stopped, and I no longer experienced these encounters with my allies.

I worked at a doctor's office during this time, and a female African American doctor, Dr. B., took an interest in me and became my mentor. She thought I was completely out of control and needed to tone down my appearance and lifestyle. I thought she had lost her mind. How dare she tell me something was wrong with how I dressed and wore my hair, nails, and hoop earrings! I was young and hardheaded, and you could not tell me that my fourteen-inch honey blonde weave and super long nails were not popping. My roommate Renee was from California and always had my hair right. My mentor boldly told me that my short skirts were a distraction and I needed to dress more appropriately at work. I went to work dressed as if I was going to a party, not a doctor's office. She knew my style and appearance would keep me from achieving my goals.

Dr. B. and I became close enough for her to tell me that I would become an educated black woman, whether I wanted to or not. She began coaching me to carry myself more professionally and how to achieve my life goals.

I began to trust Dr. B. and felt safe to share my struggles of taking care of myself without any financial support from my parents; I did not want to go back to living from piddle to post. I probably talked to my parents a few times a year and saw each of them once every year and a half or more. My new mentor could not imagine how I lived the way I did because she was a hands-on parent. Although my lifestyle was foreign to her, she didn't give up on me; she encouraged and pushed me with love.

Dr. B. invited me to her home and introduced me to her family. She began taking me to lunch outside of the office to have candid conversations about my actions. She gently suggested that I stop letting my male friends come by the office to hand me a stack of money! Instead of telling me to cut my nails, Dr. B. pointed out how their length impeded the way I cared for the infant patients. She was correct with that observation because I accidentally dropped a baby in the trash can unbeknownst to her! I thought that child's mother would kill me, but she was gracious and understanding because her daughter was uninjured!

Dr. B. was a perfect role model; she was a godsend, and I love her to this day for the light and life she breathed into me. I took heed to her advice but continue to wear my hoop earrings to this day because I like the way they look. Super cute!

Dr. B. was able to discern that I was not living up to my potential. She recognized my greatness in which I was ignoring. Knowing I was too smart to stay in that job, Dr. B. wanted to see me make better use of my capabilities and began to stand in the gap for me. When I did stupid shit, my parents would make me suffer any consequences that came my way. Dr. B. corrected and guided me when I was wrong and taught me how to do things accurately; she did not leave me to figure it out alone.

She saw an intelligent young woman who needed a reality check on aligning her goal of being a doctor to the reality of what is required. She felt I radiated enormous potential and counseled me on the requirements of attending medical school, residency, and a career as a plastic surgeon. Yes, I had dreams of becoming a plastic surgeon, but instead of focusing on my goal, I was in the streets acting like a damn fool!

Just as I was beginning to thrive and demonstrate my true capabilities with the guidance of my new mentor, a disruption came. This time, I believe it was from God, not the enemy. When Dr. B. told me I would become an educated black woman, a white female practitioner at work listened to our conversation. Several months later, the practitioner began observing me as I instructed a mother on how to do a procedure on her young child. When I finished, the practitioner called me into an office and complimented me by saying she saw how I was, maturing.

She couldn't leave it at that. Then, she said, "Not long ago, you were as ghetto as the young mother you were giving instructions to." "Dr. B. is right. You are going to become an educated nigger."

Wait, what?!

Did she say what I thought she said?

Yes, she said it. I was stunned.

It took a few days, but I decided to do something different. I advocated for myself. The practitioner was right in a sense; Dr. B.'s guidance was working. The person that God wanted me to be began to reveal her beautiful crown. I requested a meeting with the owners of the practice and shared what happened with the practitioner. The practitioner was livid because I had insisted, she be reprimanded! How dare I not accept her "compliment"! What right did I have to tell the doctors what she said to me? In her mind, she was reiterating what Dr. B. stated while in her presence. The difference was that Dr. B. referred to me as a black woman, not a nigger. The practitioner didn't see any difference in the references.

The practitioner and I spoke after I met with the owners of the practice. I told her that, despite how I carried myself, I came from an educated family. My mother had a master's degree from Columbia University and a Ph.D. in theology. My father was also a college graduate and had a successful career in aviation. I told her that my parents traveled the world and took my brothers and me with them most of the time. I informed her that I was classically trained and played the bass cello in the orchestra at a performing arts high school. I was accepted into the Atlanta Youth Symphony. I stated, with confidence and pride, that I was not a nigger. At that moment, I took full responsibility for misrepresenting myself and the educated professionals my parents were because of the pain and trauma I held onto.

Although my parents lived their lives the best way they could as young parents, they exposed my brothers and me to many things that would benefit us in the long run. I had to stop letting the enemy win. I needed to start fighting back and become the great person God intended me to be. It was time to leave my allies behind and start believing what Dr. B. saw in me; it was time to become an educated woman.

With the encouragement of my friend, I decided to leave Atlanta to accomplish this goal. Almost ten years had passed since I began struggling as a lost soul with a strong sense of unworthiness, believing the trick of the enemy instead of God. It was time to get my shit together, so I agreed to return to New York to finish college finally and move in with my mother.

Although my parents said they loved me, I felt like I was in the middle of the ocean without an anchor to keep me steady. I had to figure out life on my own. My parents had tremendous ambition and focused on their success and ability to keep themselves afloat from the world's challenges. My dad always said, "I got mine. You have to get yours." My parents were committed to their addictions. My mother's drug of choice was religion, and my father's was women.

My girlfriends had begun new chapters in their lives, having children and building their careers, when I started becoming unstuck. Once my mind became fixed on giving college another shot, a new distraction came to attempt to throw me off course! One month before I was to leave, I got arrested! *What the heck is going on, Jesus!* Why was I arrested? For a freaking traffic violation! *Unbelievable!*

One day after work, I decided to go to the mall to get some hot wings. The good hot wings were at this one spot in the mall. It was a hot summer day, so I wore a professional summer dress with lovely sling-back sandals. When I got to the mall, I noticed some police activity in the parking lot, which pricked my spirit, but I ignored it. As soon as I pulled out of the mall parking lot, hot wings in tow, I saw a police car behind me with its blue lights on. I thought,

Here we go.

I cannot afford a ticket.

I'm doing my best to save every dime I can to move to New York and go back to school. The officer pulled me over for a tag violation. Yes, I admit that my shit was raggedy as heck. The officer escorted me to the back seat of his police car. Then, he began going through my purse. *What is going on?* He asked me all kinds of crazy questions as if he was wasting time for some reason. Eventually, a white officer came over. They had a brief conversation, then the first officer who pulled me over told me I was under arrest. *Jesus, come by here!*

When I arrived at the police station, a few friendly female officers fingerprinted me, took my mugshot, and ensured my pictures were presentable. Everything got serious when a mean-ass officer came over to frisk me. She kicked my legs open, aggressively put her hand up my dress, then felt between my breasts and vagina. I was mad and humiliated at the same time and wanted to say something to defend myself so badly, but the arresting officer who witnessed the frisk shook his head in disgust and pleaded with me to be silent and listen to her commands. I complied as she threw me into an empty holding cell.

While I was sitting there trying not to catch anything I didn't need in this filthy cell, it began filling up. I was finally allowed to make my one phone call, which turned into several because none of my so-called girlfriends were willing to go to the jail to bail me out. *Are you fucking kidding me?* Finally, my cousin Bridgit showed up to bail me out, but she was told there was a federal warrant for my arrest. *What! Lord Jesus? I can't be bailed out. Huh?* I didn't know what to do or say. There was nothing Bridgit could do for me, so she left. A little while later, a sheriff told everyone in the cell that those who had not been bailed out by11:00 pm would be bound over to the county jail. *Jesus, something had to give. A miracle needed to take place!* By that time, I had been in this holding cell for about five hours.

Something had to happen quickly. Right then, a familiar face appeared. A man I often saw while hanging out in the clubs peeped his head in the window of the holding cell. As soon as I recognized him, we locked eyes. The only thing I could do was mouth the words "help me." He stared at me for a moment as if he was contemplating whether to help, then nodded his head and gestured for me to wait one minute. I must say this man did not have to help me at all. When we would see each other at the nightclub, he would ask me to dance and wanted my number, but I always respectfully declined. The man I never gave a chance to get to know me turned out to be the miracle I needed.

Several minutes passed, then the officers began removing the women from my holding cell and escorting them to the county jail. They told me I was staying in the cell because I was being held for the Marshals to come and expedite me. After that loud public announcement, a woman taking up the entire bench looked at me and sucked her teeth. Rolling her eyes, she said, "It's always the bougie ones who do the real criminal shit!" I looked back at her in a way for her to understand if she tried me, I would fuck her up. It seemed she had let my professional attire fool her!

The man from the club, who happened to be at work early that night, came toward me and said I'd have to stay longer. It would be a while because he had to run cross checks to make sure I was the person they had the warrant for. He asked for my date of birth and social security number, then disappeared once again. I prayed and searched my mind for anything I could have done to get myself into this situation. Nothing major came to mind.

When the officer returned, he told me that I was clear to go! It turns out someone had stolen my identity. Once I was arrested, no one checked to make sure I was the person the warrant was issued for. That is until my angel arrived to save me. *Hallelujah! Thank you, Jesus! Amen!* I thanked him from the bottom of my heart because I understood the magnitude of his graciousness to help me. Then, it seemed that he had disappeared into thin air! I never saw him again after that fateful night.

When I looked at the clock, it was 10:50 p.m., precisely ten minutes before the deadline to move to the county jail and change into an orange jumpsuit! The ladies who were releasing me from custody jokingly asked what I had been doing at that mall. They said it was a crime trap; police swept every day to catch people who did not have their tags or registration in place. Poverty is expensive!

I returned to work and tried to act as nothing had happened, but I told a coworker about my ordeal because I needed her to help me get my car out of the impound lot. She asked if I had told Dr. B. what had happened. After this, I was compelled to call Dr. B. to tell her about the horrible mess I had gotten myself into. Petrified when I called her, she was the perfect mentor and instructed me to tell the doctors I worked for what happened because my coworker would not keep this information to herself. For this reason, I had to be the one in control of my narrative. This was when I learned that I always had to maintain control of my story. I should never leave it to an outside party to tell someone something detrimental about me. If I told my truth, I controlled the narrative. I carry this lesson with me to this day.

I had to go to court for the tag violation. Knowing I could not go to court without an attorney, I called my parents to tell them that I had been arrested and asked if they would help me obtain one. Neither of them agreed to help me, so I was left to problem solve on my own. Eager to change my situation, I called my father's sister, my Aunt Debbie. She agreed to help me and paid for my attorney. Boy, was I grateful to her for her love and support at that pivotal time. Without her, my goal to go back to college would have gone down the drain.

When I finally arrived in New York to pay my college fees, I was informed that I had to pay more than earlier quoted to start the semester. *Fuck it. I know my parents are not going to help me, so I might as well go back to Atlanta.* My Aunt Debbie did not see it that way.

She gave me the money to start school because, at some point, I needed help from someone; she was my saving grace.

The encouragement and guidance from Dr. B., the unconditional love and financial support from my aunt, and the fact that my mother agreed to let my grown ass come live with her, were the anchors I needed to succeed, and they showed up in the nick of time. An anchor is a person who is willing to hold you down in challenging times and keep you steady. Life can be rocky as hell, and it is crucial to have people in your life to embrace you and say, "I got you!"

God always knows what you need when you need it. If I had to do it over again, I would have reached for the anchors in my life much sooner. I would not have attempted to struggle in silence despite my parents' absence in my teen and young adult years. I should have held on to my friend's mothers tighter because they were my anchors during the dark times. I was too blind, feeling like I was a burden. Aunt Juanita clothed me! Mama Dee provided shelter for me! and Mama Lynn nurtured me! They were there to save me the entire time, and trust me, they did! I understand now that everyone isn't your friend. However, God placed three girlfriends in my life so that their mothers could stand in the gap for me when my parents were unable to. It was all part of His plan.

CHRONICLE VII
MY HEART OR MY HABIT

Moving back to New York was perfect for my soul. I was finally able to move in a productive direction. I lived with my mom and was progressing well as a nontraditional student. I began meeting like-minded people, including my line sisters, who were nine years younger than me. These women changed my life! They were academically and socially balanced, something I was unaccustomed to while attending school in Atlanta. In my eyes, they were babies, but they were focused on doing well in school, studying abroad, participating in extracurricular activities, working jobs, and becoming a part of a sorority. Inspired, I stepped up my game to be part of that tribe.

Because I was many years older than them, my line sisters lovingly called me "Grand ma ma," and my mom was "Rev ma ma." Once we began our process, they were at my house every single night for about six months. Around the third month, my mom left us at her apartment and moved to take care of her ailing father. My soul began to heal during this time. My line sisters motivated me in a way that my inner strength began to grow as God's destiny for my life started to reveal itself in a way that I could not deny.

One of the beautiful things about becoming a part of an organized group is that you can link up with people that you may in ordinary circumstances never cross paths with. For me, my sisters of Naughty 9 were godsends, and I will always love them for it. Spending three and a half years in New York to get my life on track was the best decision I could have made. I developed the most beautiful friendships I have ever had with males as well. My relationships in Atlanta vs. New York made it clear how my broken soul kept me trapped in broken relationships. The healthy friendships that I was creating were refreshing and much needed.

Before leaving Atlanta, I was convinced that Brandon was my heart. I should have let him go, but I could not overcome trying to hold on to familiar relationships for dear life regardless of their value. It was easy to continue being with him because he was not abusive or disrespectful on the surface; he was extremely good at making me feel I could put my guard down with him. How could I have been so naïve and ignored all the red flags that God presented while I was discovering a better me? Brandon was good at hiding his true self. God wanted to free me as the walls of my trauma bonds were crumbling, but I refused to accept what He was doing in my life. I was so damn hard-headed! I stayed with this man out of habit. All the signs were there!

One time, Brandon called me two days after I met one of the finest men in the world. He and I had not spoken to each other for several months because he was too busy playing the field and spending all his money in the streets while I was getting my life together. Then, that damn devil put Brandon back in my face after he had been out of sight out of mind. After I got off the phone with the cutie pie, Brandon called with his classic, "what you doing?" phrase. He proceeded to tell me that he had recently been evicted! I should have hung up on his ass, but I didn't! I listened to his sob story instead of kicking him back to the curb.

After a few more phone calls, I agreed to see Brandon again after he confessed his "love" only because he had nowhere to go and no one to turn to other than my broken soul. He needed to be rescued, and I was his target. By New Year's Eve of that year, he called and suggested that we get married. It was about 3 a.m. I was asleep and thought he was playing. I called him back on New Year's Day to ask if he was serious about getting married. He played it off and said he was joking, but he also said he would marry me if I asked him to. To this day, he still says I asked him to get married.

We moved forward with this marriage idea after dating on and off for seven years. When I told my mother I was getting married, she pretty much cussed me out. Looking back, I can't be mad because she had not even met this man. Brandon had not met my brothers, father, Aunt Debbie, or my line sisters. He knew nobody in my life! Plus, he did not get me a ring.

After graduating, I moved back to Atlanta so that Brandon and I could prepare for our upcoming nuptials the following summer. This fool had an entire year to get his shit together. Instead of getting a new apartment for us to share, he moved in with his father; I acted like nothing was wrong with that. Until this point, I had never lived with a man and knew this was something I would not do until I got married. When I first moved out after high school graduation, my father told me to never let a man think he was paying your rent and never give a man the keys to your apartment, so I never did. Since Brandon and I were planning to get married, I agreed to move in with him.

Brandon drove a nice, tricked-out car and had a clean apartment when I left Atlanta three years earlier. When I returned to Atlanta, Brandon drove his dad's old, raggedy Buick and only had a mattress on the floor. It was clear that his lifestyle had changed for the worse; he needed to be saved from himself. What was I thinking? Why didn't I run for the hills? I had grown so much only to go backward.

That Valentine's Day, Brandon took me out to dinner to officially pop the question. This time, with a ring. I knew something was up because he was nervous from the time he came home from work. The restaurant is super crowded, so we decided to have dinner at the bar. *This fool knew he was going to propose and should have waited for a table.* I reluctantly agreed to eat at the bar because I knew he was going to propose. For some reason, I felt afraid, not excited. My spirit told me something was off; this wasn't going to turn out well. Brandon and I ordered our food at the bar, then nervously started making small talk. It felt like I was sitting with a stranger. When our food arrived, we ate in silence.

Once we were close to finishing our meals, Brandon awkwardly reached for his jacket pocket and began to pull out a small, black velvet box. Looking scared to death but smiling at the same time, Brandon finally opened the ring box and asked if I would marry him. As much as the feeling of doom was stirring in my spirit, I thought maybe seeing the ring would change my mind. *Nope, that ring was so freakin small I could not even see the diamond!* Looking at the ring, I began to feel a tremendous sense of disappointment. The feeling was so overwhelming that I had to excuse myself and go to the ladies' room. While there, I stared at the ring Brandon gave me and did my best to fix my face and find some level of excitement. Grasping that I could not even fake feeling disappointed, I returned to Brandon at the bar. He's talking to a lovely woman who is smiling and appears to be excited about our engagement. She politely said "Congratulations" and asked to see my ring. Embarrassed to show her my ring, *I rolled my eyes and said, no, mind your business!* Brandon knew it was time to go!

The next day, I tried my best to rationalize why I should accept Brandon's ring. I called a few friends and even called my father, who told me not to worry about it. *Why the hell did I even try to ask my father? He could care less what I deserved as a woman or as his daughter.*

Ultimately, I told Brandon to take the ring back and save more money to get a better one. I know I hurt his feelings, but I knew I was worth more than this chip of a ring he had presented. I should have walked away at that point. I could hear God's voice, but I refused to honor Him when it came to this relationship. The wounds of the enemy were embedded in my heart; I did not possess the courage to break the curse of pain. Instead of calling off the wedding or sitting down with Brandon to discuss our expectations for our marriage, I passively moved ahead, knowing we were not meant to be married to each other.

Burying my head in the sand, I moved forward with the wedding plans and sent out the invitations. Adding insult to my madness, I had the audacity to have seventeen girls in my wedding party! I had eleven bridesmaids and six hostesses! My mother paid for the entire wedding! My father contributed as well, but despite my stupidity, my mother took care of everything. The wedding was beautiful, and my Atlanta friends did not miss the opportunity to act like pure fools. They argued so much that they forgot to bring the unity candles and marriage certificate to the church. Denise talked about me so badly on the way to the reception that my friend, Cella, was ready to kick her ass.

My mother did an awesome job putting my wedding together. Everything was top-notch! What did Brandon's family do? Nothing! No one in his family attended our wedding. His father, who he was very close with and lived with, didn't say boo about it. He did not even show up. His mother who told me her son wasn't ready for marriage came because I purchased her ticket to New York and gave her the dress to wear for the occasion. *Shit! Someone from his side of the family had to be there.*

What was I going to tell everyone if nobody from Brandon's family was there? What a ridiculous decision! *Fuck the red flags. I was going to marry this man even though it was clear he was not ready.* He was broke. *Check. His* family did not support the marriage. *Check.* I did not have a ring. *Check.* He only met my parents once before the wedding. *Check.* I knew I should not marry him. *Check.* I believed the enemy instead of God about him. *Check.*

I tried to be optimistic about my marriage to Brandon after the wedding. My godmother Lynn and Dr. B. encouraged me to hang in there and offered excellent guidance on being a good wife and dealing with the ups and downs. These beautiful women based their advice on the fact that Brandon was at least doing his part. Unfortunately, he only did the bare minimum.

When I finally adjusted to living in Atlanta again, I pulled myself together and got a job in my field. After about a year or so, we eventually moved into our own apartment. I bought a car and began executing my plan to buy a house. We lived in the apartment for about a year before I started the process of buying our first home. The wonderful thing about Atlanta at that time was the average person could afford to build a home in a nice community from the ground up; that is what I did.

Every weekend, my high school friend, Charles, and I went looking high and low for the perfect location of my new home. We remained close over the years, and both decided to settle in Atlanta after finishing school. Since Charles purchased a home the year before, he offered to show me the ropes. You would think Brandon would have been a part of this process, but he wasn't. If he was not at work, he was at the apartment watching sports. When I found a location to build our home, I took Brandon to see the model home. He said he liked it, so I selected the lot to build it on. By the following summer, the house was ready for us to move in. That was all the input I received from him.

Attempting to be the perfect wife, I tried to make a way for us and our soon-to-be family, or so I thought. Once the house was finished, Brandon told me that his father was moving in with us. I emphatically disagreed. I had already mapped out how our new home would look, and his father was not part of the equation. Especially since I went to his father before buying our house to ask if he wanted to live with us, he declined after I assured him it would be ok. Knowing I opened my heart to him before starting the home buying process, I stood my ground, closed on the house, got the keys, and left town to go to the Essence Festival in New Orleans to celebrate with my friends. When I returned from my trip,

Brandon and I moved into our home. His father didn't speak to me for nearly ten years after that.

It started becoming obvious that Brandon was my habit, and we did not romantically love each other. I confused my need to ensure a stable life by financially supporting myself and having a home to call my own with someone I was comfortable with, as love for my husband. In truth, my husband was merely coming along for the ride; he had no intention of providing or protecting. I was not his heart; I was his habit.

CHRONICLE VIII
WE CAN BE TOO LOYAL TO OUR DECISIONS

We can often be too loyal to the decisions we make in our lives. I got married knowing it was a mistake, and instead of changing course, I remained faithful to my decision. Not getting married would have been the best choice for my life. I was grinding to ensure a better life and praying that Brandon would come through as a husband to provide the things we needed. It was no big deal if we could not afford things; we would keep pushing to get what we needed.

Just like any other married couple, we had bills. My husband thought our mortgage was too much for him, and he should not have to pay it. I knew I never wanted to have to rely on someone else for a place to live ever again, so I did what I had to do to keep a roof over my head. This situation taught me that if a man does not love you enough to provide for you, there is nothing you can say to convince him otherwise.

A woman from the mortgage company contacted us whenever we were late to make a payment. She always wanted Brandon to be on the call and took the time to coach and guided us on what we should do to maintain our home and enhance our lives. That woman did not know us from Adam, but she took the time to breathe life into our marriage and offer guidance on adequately managing our finances. I believe this was a God thing. It was clear that this woman was rooting for us and wanted us to win. Unfortunately, Brandon did not. He had no aspirations to succeed as my husband and could care less about what this woman had to say to us and was adamant about not paying the mortgage. Even when I offered a solution for him to pay half of the mortgage on time, Brandon's position was that he wasn't paying anything.

Three years into our marriage, I became an entrepreneur and started a nonprofit. While running this grassroots organization, my income was inconsistent. When I did not make any money, many of our household bills were not paid on time. I had a husband who worked every day, but my life consisted of constantly making payment arrangements. I will tell you this; the cable bill was paid. Our bill was at least $500-$600 a month, and Brandon paid that shit on time, every month! Despite my husband's lackluster effort to be a provider, I kept grinding no matter what. We did not have children yet, so it was no big deal. During this time, I understood that God was wholeheartedly my provider.

I had two back surgeries in four years, and God truly kept it together for me. The first surgery happened a year after Brandon, and I moved into our new home. He did take care of me during this time and made sure to have food for me when he got home from work. I could not walk or stand up straight. I was in complete agony. Four years later, after my second back surgery, I ultimately released my suffering to God and began fervently praying for my physical healing. Gratefully, the Lord answered my prayers, and I became pregnant after my second back surgery.

Two months before finding out I was pregnant, one of my former students, Gugu, called to share that she had a dream. In her dream, God revealed to her that I was having a boy. I thanked her for sharing her vision, but I knew I was not having a baby. I was well into my forties by this time. I tried to convince Brandon to adopt, but he was adamantly against it.

A few months after Gugu's call, my mother visited me for Thanksgiving. When I drove to the bus station on the shady side of town, I decided to wait for her in my car to avoid getting a ticket. When my mother finally got into the car, we gave each other long hugs. As soon as we pulled out of the bus station, my mother took a long look at me and asked if I was okay. I shrugged my shoulders and told her that I was. After we arrived at my house, my mother asked me a second time if I was okay. Again, I said to her that I was.

Earlier that day, my girlfriend, Felicitia, called and told me that she had a dream of a baby in my house. At this point, I had about eight or nine godchildren who always came to visit or stay with me, so it was not unusual for children to be in my home. Felicitia then stated that the baby she dreamt about was mine. I told her the same thing I said to Gugu: I was too old to have a baby. Then, she reminded me that I'd been talking about my "cycle starting soon" for the last two months.

After catching up, my mom and I went to the grocery store to pick up some items for Thanksgiving dinner the next day. While at the store, I picked up a ten-pound bag of ice. When I turned to put it in the cart, I noticed that lifting the ice hurt my lower stomach a little. After we got home, I felt a slight pain in my lower belly. I thought, *Why the fuck am I having abdominal pain? Is my husband messing around with another woman? Did he give me something?*

I woke up early on Thanksgiving morning to the smell of a perfectly cooked turkey in the oven. While lying in bed and looking up at the white popcorn ceiling, I thought about the abdominal pain I was still experiencing. Immediately, I jumped straight up in the bed and told myself to take a pregnancy test.

My girlfriend, Kish, and I had a running joke about buying a pregnancy test from the dollar store. I took them periodically because, since I suffered from polycystic ovary syndrome, I did not have a cycle for months at a time. I took pregnancy tests, hoping one would tell me I was pregnant, but they were always negative.

This time, I quietly went into the bathroom while Brandon was sleeping. He had just gotten home after working the night shift. I went to my bathroom's linen closet, found my dollar store test, and proceeded to pee on the stick. I was nervous as hell for some reason, feeling like a teenager who was about to find out her fate. While waiting for the result, I told myself that the test would be negative; I would tell my girlfriends that their dreams were not about me.

When I looked at the test in my hand, I saw two pink lines! *Oh. My. GOD! This can't be right. Am I pregnant? What am I going to do?* I felt like I was sixteen and nervous as fuck! *Is there a baby inside of me for real? Lord, help me!*

After a few more minutes of convincing myself that I was pregnant, having an entire conversation inside my head, I quietly went back into the bedroom and gently shook Brandon's bare arm. He didn't respond. I shook him harder, and he rumbled in his sleep a little before turning over to ignore me. I pushed him and told him to wake up because I was trying to show him the stick at the same time.

Groggy, he said, "What? Why are you waking me up? I'm sleeping!"

I answered, "Wake up, boy! I'm pregnant!"

He replied, "Dang! Why did you wake me up?" Then, without missing a beat, he said, "Don't tell nobody." In my best, *don't let me slap the shit out of you* voice, I responded, "What? Don't tell nobody?!" He said, "Yeah." Then, he turned over and went back to sleep. *I know this mother fucker did not act like I told him to go to the store or something.* Rolling my eyes, I went upstairs to wake my mother up from her sleep to share the news with her. Entering the guest bedroom, I called, "Ma!" "Ma!"

When she woke up, I put the pregnancy test in her face. My mother was as blind as a bat, so she did not see what I had put in front of her. Anxious and excited, I finally yelled, "I'm pregnant! It took her a few minutes to process my announcement, but then she held her heart and took in my blessing.

I am so grateful my mother was there to share that moment with me. After saying a short prayer, she came downstairs. I began calling my family to tell them the good news. I especially could not wait to call my cousins, Krissie and Thulie. One Thursday, when we were on our weekly call together while watching *Grey's Anatomy*, I mentioned that I had missed my period. Thulie said I was going through menopause! Thank the Lord I was having a bundle of joy instead! What a wonderful memory.

Brandon continued to work every day, yet he still only contributed a small amount of money to the household. Again, I realized I should have abandoned my decision to marry him. Once our son, BJ, was born, paying the bills became a struggle for me. Making mortgage payments on time became harder and harder; we got to the point where we were at risk of losing our home. For a minute, I considered letting the house go and moving into an apartment. I even began looking for one, but God had other plans.

About two months before the confrontation with Brandon, when he confessed to having sex with escorts, I got a call from the woman from our mortgage company. She was livid. She proceeded to tell me how disappointed she was with us; she could not believe that we were on the brink of foreclosure. She went so far as to say, if I had a husband who was unwilling to pay his mortgage, I needed to get rid of him. I wanted to cry, but there were too many people in front of me. I was in the middle of a business meeting when I took her call. As usual, I held it together and followed the woman's instructions to make an immediate mortgage payment.

I was in New York on a business trip and didn't know where anything was in that part of Manhattan. By the grace of God, when I stepped outside of my hotel, there was my bank directly across the street. After making the payment, I felt disgusted with myself and could barely speak until I saw my son, who was staying with my family in Queens while I worked in the city. As I held my son, I knew it was time to make a change; I needed to let go of the loyalty of my decision to marry Brandon. Sometimes you must get out of the way and allow God to come in and give you something far greater than you imagined for yourself.

Having the courage to let go of prior choices is as important as having the courage to move forward. In my case, God told me to do both. I had to let Brandon go and move forward in my life. I took responsibility for my part in the dysfunction that I allowed to take place fifteen years before Brandon's confession. In my healing, I have learned that I am not obligated to have someone in my life just because they ask. The same goes for you. If the person's attributes do not serve you in a way that uplifts and supports you, it is okay to say, *Thanks, but no thanks.* It doesn't make you a bad person. It means you have the courage and strength to trust God for what He wants for your life.

I am loyal to a fault. It was important to free myself of several individuals I felt obligated to remain attached to because of the time I had known them. I had to let go of my need to be loyal to people who did not deserve it. With my husband, I confused storage/familiar love because of the time we spent dating. Understanding that Brandon did not deserve my hand in marriage was healing in itself. I encourage you to muster the courage to let go of the things that do not serve you. When you make a decision and later find that you made a mistake, it is absolutely okay to save yourself and change course and create a better path for your life.

CHRONICLE IX
DAMN, IT WAS A TRAUMA BOND!

My healing process led me to question why I was complicit in a relationship with Brandon. It was time to face what I viewed as the difference between loving someone and having a trauma bond with that person. My husband wanted me, but he did not love me. When you love someone, you have profoundly tender affection for them; you are willing to sacrifice your wants and needs to meet your partner's needs. Your love for the other person gives you the patience required to work through the trials and tribulations that unfold during the relationship. Remember, "Love does not delight in evil but rejoices with the truth. It always protects, always trust, always hopes, always perseveres." (New International Version 1 Corinthians 13:6-7).

Realizing that a man has never truly loved me was sobering and admitting that I never loved any of the men in my life in return was a hard pill to swallow. This epiphany forced me to come to grips with how lonely I was in my marriage and past relationships. Carrying on as a successful career woman, mother, and friend and behaving as though I was not constantly enduring love trauma within my marriage was my modus operandi. Pretending nothing was amiss in my soul had to come to an end, and forgiveness needed to come forward. It was time to be honest about my trauma surrounding love so that I could begin to gain the courage to open my heart and receive love.

By being honest about my love trauma, I realized that my loveless "situation-ships" were a manifestation of my relationship with my parents. During therapy, I faced the fact that my father had no clue how to raise a young woman and did not teach me how to love myself. I'm sure he thought he was doing the right thing by teaching me how to provide for myself, be independent, cook, and clean. This man ruled with an iron fist and prioritized teaching me the hard skills I needed to get through this cruel world.

Being raised by a Marine required daily practice drills on not asking anyone for help. My critical thinking and problem-solving skills have been on point since I was in middle school. The barking of instructions made me a strong-minded person with a hard exterior, but the lack of nurturing did not give me a chance to figure out how to love others warmly. I approached many relationships with masculine energy that always threw people off.

My father lectured me on what I needed to do to get and keep a man. This usually included learning how to cook, clean, and satisfy a man's needs. I know this is all true and important as a grown woman, but these informative lessons didn't teach me how to love a man. With love as the missing link, my relationships were unfulfilling. I was with people who desired me, but they did not love or nurture me. This is most likely why my marriage ended after my husband decided he was no longer attracted to me. There was no love to hold on to, to keep us together through the trials and challenging times. The healing in this lesson meant I could forgive Brandon's severe betrayal because, in the grand scheme of things, it was his loss of desire, not love, that flat-lined our marriage and ultimately gave me the clarity to walk away and never turn back.

Healing gave me the courage to reject the people who did not nurture and love me in a manner that I deserved. I began to enter friendships filled with reciprocity of love, respect, and kindness with people who genuinely cared for me and were concerned about my well-being. This applied to every relationship in my life: professional, romantic, platonic, and familial. My soul began to reject relationships that did not make me feel safe or appreciated.

Identifying the role, I played in my marriage also led me to understand that the destruction of my relationship was not entirely my fault. Instead of looking in the mirror and facing their trauma, the person at fault usually blames or finds reasons in their partner why they have betrayed them. Brandon continued his awful behavior even after our marriage ended. As a co-parent, he continued to put himself first and never made the sacrifices necessary to provide and protect. He left me hanging with the family's needs and was only financially responsible when convenient for him.

Despite his antics, I will say that Brandon was great when spending time with BJ. It was important to me that BJ had a strong relationship with his dad. I selfishly wanted never to let Brandon see me and BJ again, but I put my ego aside and allowed their father-son relationship to develop. This decision was not in vain because Brandon and BJ have a beautiful relationship. BJ thinks his father is a superhero, but he does not yet realize that his mother is the one who holds the shield.

Society suggests that you should go to therapy to deal with past issues, but no one tells you about the harsh realities and pain your soul will endure in the self-discovery process. This healing process can be tough; accepting my childhood's role in how I viewed myself was hard to deal with. The creases of my pain ran deeper than I wanted to admit, but I needed to uncover another layer of why I created trauma bonds in the place of loving relationships.

To start, I tried to talk to my father about my feelings, hoping to address the high school graduation day incident and the way he viciously attacked me. As usual, he continued the trauma and cussed me out so severely that I hung up the damn phone. *What a way to teach your daughter how to be treated!*

My experience with my mother was no better. I don't know why my mother pined over my father for so long. She continued to love him even though he had remarried twice by the time I had BJ. Pushing me to go to him on her behalf and having him curse my ass out and tell me to mind my business every time I went to him was always traumatic for me. While my mother was in a jealous rage about my father refusing to speak to her, she would say extremely hurtful things to me that completely broke my heart.

Our interactions were so tumultuous at times. I often suggested that she and I go to counseling together, but she always told me, "All I need is Jesus." Counseling can help people work through a myriad of life's difficulties, and I genuinely wish we could have gone together while we had the chance. But my mother was deeply religious and old school; she believed in praying her way through her sufferings.

As if I hadn't endured enough, my parents' painful pricks continued during my separation from Brandon, which was utterly devastating. When Brandon called my father to tell him what happened (before I could), I thought my father would finally come to my rescue. Boy, was I sadly mistaken. My father came over to our house, sat on the couch next to me, then proceeded to tell Brandon that he could always call him if he ever needed to talk to somebody. He understood what Brandon was going through and would not judge him. *Are you fucking kidding me!* Once again, my father didn't take the opportunity to nurture me and protect my heart. Comforting and showing compassion for me as his daughter would have given me the self-assurance that I needed to push through the traumatic experience with my husband more boldly.

As if taking Brandon's side was not awful enough, my father called me a few weeks later to say that I was to blame for the horrible things my husband did. I had not been a good wife because I was trying to succeed in my career. *What planet was this man living on? What century was it?* I held the book of matches and was ready to strike them to burn the relationship bridge with my father forever.

In counseling, I learned to forgive the people who played essential roles in my life and began to live without fear of rejection and distrust. Although the relationships that were supposed to be my anchors were completely crumbling my heart, it was paramount to figure out how to make a healthy transition to live my life with love and joy. The misconception I had regarding love was a challenging revelation, but it helped me grasp that I was suffering from a level of dysfunction that I had normalized since my childhood. I did not want to pass this unhealthy behavior on to my love doves (the children I adore).

Breaking this cycle would help me break the curse and prevent generational wounds in my children. Teaching my babies how to have healthy, loving relationships was necessary due to the trauma I experienced growing up and into adulthood. I wanted my love doves to experience love and nurturing through my practical example; they needed to know with great confidence that I would protect them from and address any family trauma they may face. I did not want them to question my love for them, especially when the time came for discipline and correction.

Teach children how to trust you and your intentions. Help them identify the anchor relationships in their lives. The onset of distrust and trauma is an inevitable life experience but addressing them with your children and loved ones is crucial. Ignoring trauma can lead young people to connect with the wrong crowd or enter abusive relationships. Based on my upbringing, I was a classic case for mistaking trauma bonds as love; this happened with my husband. According to Rhonda Richards-Smith, "The experiences we have as children bonding with a caretaker shape how we maintain a bond with a romantic partner. If your childhood was filled with abuse and trauma, you will be attracted to that in a partner and a relationship because it is how you understand love."[1] Brandon reinforced the trauma I experienced while growing up, being taught not to expect to receive help or support from anyone else.

Before my healing journey began, I would not have identified myself as being in an abusive marriage. Looking back, I was to some degree. Brandon had very little to say to me. Not doing things together as a married couple was a form of emotional abuse and manipulation. I ultimately accepted it because the silence was the opposite of the verbal attacks I received from my father. Verbal attacks from men are emotional triggers for me, so I went from one extreme to another. I normalized my husband's silence and unwillingness to provide, which was my baggage, not Brandon's. I now own my role in letting this type of treatment slide and not addressing my trauma earlier in my life.

When you know better, you do better. It was time to implement strategies to help me reach a healthy place of love and restoration after my

---

[1] Amer-Marie. "Are You Really In Love Or Just Trauma Bonding?" (XO NECOLE, 21 Nov. 2020.)

marriage. Creating trauma bonds with individuals was a coping mechanism I learned at an early age, and it was natural to me. Being raised by a man who never let his emotional guard down with his daughter and a mother who dramatically expressed the loss of love was all I knew. To this day, I continue to struggle to break this pattern due to my familiarity with narcissistic individuals because my parents were so self-centered when it came to their emotional needs. To a fault, I was passive-aggressive when it came to my needs during my marriage. I often wonder if my husband viewed me as a meek pussycat or as a strong lioness. The way he behaved; it seems he thought I was a pussycat.

CHRONICLE X
THE PUSSYCAT VS. THE LIONESS

Contrary to my own belief, I played the role of the pussycat versus the lioness. I had grown into the lioness that I knew I was while resetting my life in New York. When I returned to Atlanta, I took on the gentle, easy-going persona instead of modeling my fierce, intense, passionate, and beautiful lioness spirit. Instead of empowering Brandon, I enabled him. I own that.

By playing the role of the pussycat, I allowed his unacceptable behavior and poor decisions to slide. I should have checked Brandon on that Thanksgiving morning when he ignored me after telling him I was pregnant with his child. I kept it moving as usual and did not realize how fucked up his reaction was. I wasn't some one-night stand or a casual girlfriend; I was his wife of twelve years! We waited for a long time to become parents, and he reacted as if I was annoying him. I often wondered why my husband never came to me to express his excitement about becoming a father. Looking back, it seemed we never shared the same delight about having a child. I felt like he became disconnected during my pregnancy.

Brandon came to the initial perinatologist visit, but I went to most of the other doctor's visits alone. At the time, I never thought anything of it because I was accustomed to doing important things solo. When it was time to find out the sex of the baby, I insisted that Brandon attend the doctor's visit with me. I didn't want to experience this special occasion without him. Brandon and I did not talk to each other under the best circumstances, so he rarely had much to say by this time.

Once inside the exam room, Brandon made small talk with the sonogram technician as she prepared to do the procedure. I held my breath in complete silence when the tech squirted the warm gel on my belly and began rolling the sonogram tool around my stomach. As she paused to take pictures, it seemed like an entire hour passed before she was finally ready to reveal the sex of the baby. After a long pause, she said, "It's a boy!" Hearing those words filled me with overwhelming joy. God had spoken to me early in my pregnancy to say I was having a boy. I also had a vision of how this beautiful blessing was going to look; he was perfect. When the technician announced the sex of the baby, my first thought was that God is so real because the confirmation of His word came forth. With this reassurance, I began to cry tears of joy and felt His anointing all over me.

Weeping silently, I looked over at Brandon. I was convinced that this would be the moment we would connect. Brandon always wanted to have a son by a certain age. To share this beautiful moment, I turned to Brandon for an embrace, but this mother fucker didn't even look my way! He did not say a single word to me. He did not get up from his chair to wipe a tear from my face, rub my shoulder, give a gentle kiss, or anything.

I got nothing. This disconnected idiot took out his phone and called his father to share our exciting news with him. As I continued to weep on the exam table, I watched him share his answered prayers of having a boy with his father. At that moment, I played the role of the pussycat and quietly let the feeling of hurt come upon me and steal my joy.

Why didn't I lash out with the strength of a lioness? Why didn't I transform into a vicious female dog and bitch slap his ass for being so inconsiderate and acting like I wasn't in the room? It was so important for me to stay calm and healthy. I did not let the lioness come to the surface when I would have been justified in my actions.

Again, my healing journey has allowed me to own my passive behavior and attribute it to the sense of unworthiness I was battling because that was the trick, I allowed the enemy to use against me to hold my greatness at bay. This was an internal issue that had nothing to do with Brandon. He was the beneficiary of my baggage, not the cause.

After becoming a parent, I continued playing the role of a pussycat by letting my husband get away with not doing his household duties because I was trained to take care of myself, which benefited my husband. He did not pay the mortgage, buy baby formula, go to the supermarket to get groceries, or anything, a complete husband violation on every level, and I enabled Brandon to do very little for his family. The writing was on the wall, and I could not ignore it any longer. Becoming a mother urged the lioness to come forward to protect her cub. It was the rise of the lioness that woke me up and brought forth the awareness to move in my strength and ask my husband for a divorce a year after our son was born. Brandon ignored my request even though he knew he had a deep dark secret, and of course I let it go, although my gut was telling me not too!

The Mother's Day before BJ turned two years old; I planned to take him on vacation to visit friends in Jamaica. Brandon insisted on going. I warned him that I would not pay for his flight, and he had to put up his half to go on the trip. I attempted to play the lioness role and put my foot down on Brandon's bullshit, but he played the maudlin role so well. He acted so fucking pitiful that I punked out and paid for his ticket to go on my trip. BJ and I stayed in Jamaica for two weeks. Brandon stayed for one and talked about renewing our vows with family and friends in Jamaica. His aspirations to renew our vows still were not enough for him to kiss me, flirt, or make a pass at me. He didn't try to pull on my panties or reach for me in any way. We did not have sex not one time while in Jamaica on vacation, and I noticed.

Toward the end of my marriage to Brandon, I became a lioness and handled balancing my career as a CEO in a male-dominated industry and a new mother. I traveled for work with my son, came home to take care of Brandon's father, taking him to the hospital or for doctor's visits, and kept the household intact all at the same time. I put my suspicions about my husband on the shelf. Each time I noticed something out of order with him, I pushed it to the back of my mind. I saw the new underwear. I noticed him leaving for work early. I was aware that he never had any money even after I knew he had gotten paid. We still slept in the same bed together every night like nothing was wrong. Addressing my suspicions would have been a distraction to what was more important in my eyes, taking care of my family's needs.

After our first or second year of marriage, I promised myself that I would not become paranoid about my husband cheating. I did not look through his things or call him while he was at work. I only went to his job unannounced once, twice tops. I knew that God would reveal it to me if something were wrong. I knew that I would have to be prepared for the consequences if and when I went looking for something. *Henceforth that pill bottle!*

BJ was a few months old when I found the pill bottle. I knew Brandon and I were not having sex, but I wasn't prepared to walk away. A month before we went to Jamaica, I planned a staycation and made reservations at the Ritz Carlton for my birthday. We did not get a babysitter, so we took BJ with us. When we arrived, Brandon said he would pay for the room. His credit card declined, so I had to cover the room for him.

On top of that, we did not have sex. The next day, Brandon claimed he had to take care of some business and disappeared for hours. I decided to take in the day, so I put BJ in his stroller and took a stroll around downtown Atlanta. During our walk, I wondered what was taking Brandon so long. I also reminded myself to start paying closer attention to how Brandon moved, so I did.

Months before Brandon's confession, I began having vivid dreams about his infidelity. When I woke up, I tried to shake it off. We were sharing one car, and I dropped Brandon off at work. One job site he was on was across the street from a strip club. Whenever I dropped Brandon off, I always got an eerie feeling about that place. No matter how hard I tried, I could never rationalize why I felt so uncomfortable there. I knew Brandon liked porn, but I did not think he would be so stupid to throw his money away on strippers. It turns out I was the stupid one!

He had become so irresponsible with spending his money on women that it could no longer be ignored. An incident happened as the warning shot needed to ensure that the rug that hid all Brandon's deceitful shenanigans had been rolled back once and for all. Brandon had come to the airport to pick me and BJ up after one of my trips. As we were waiting in the cashier line to exit the parking lot, Brandon pulled out a zip lock bag of nickels. *What in the loose change is going on!* My soul was stinging with humiliation. Brandon should have just knocked me on the head with the bag of coins; that is how mortified I was feeling. In complete disgust, I looked at my husband, feeling embarrassed and saying to myself, "It's *time to deal with his trifling ass!*"

My pussycat tendencies saved my husband's life many times, but I was aware of the sneaky things men were capable of doing behind a woman's back. Being raised with all men gave me a front seat to the womanizing shenanigans men did, and Brandon was no different. He escaped the wrath of my robust and assertive nature by being quiet and non-confrontational. His disposition rarely triggered my internal alarms to let me know something was wrong. He was an expert at staying under the radar, which I learned was a manipulation tactic. Brandon understood my strength and knew how to play against it in a way that solely served himself.

Taking responsibility for moving back to Atlanta to marry, knowing my relationship with Brandon had crumbled long before initially leaving Atlanta, is easy because God loved me enough to bless me to become a mother before my marriage ended. Discovering the love God wanted for me led me to have the courage to stop diminishing my value and pursue what was destined for my life. Playing the pussycat ultimately got me to the love that my mother first revealed to me on the eve of my graduation. God's love was in me the entire time and held me until I could find my way through the pain and tell my story with dignity and grace.

Sharing my healing journey will prayerfully prevent other people from falling for the same tricks of the enemy. Since I have the opportunity to share my missteps with you, I can tell you that you can change the narrative of your life. There aren't any rules or reasons to remain in a situation that does not serve you. It's your life, so you get to set the rules and standards that work for you. If you are in your 20's, 30's, 40's, 50's, 60's, or beyond, make the adjustments in your life that bring you joy and love. Maintain a firm understanding of God's love and what He wants for you. Knowing your worth is necessary to your self-dignity and wholeness.

When someone tells you something that isn't true about yourself, you sense it immediately. We can feel the lie in our souls, so don't let them repeat it. Reject the lies and tricks because the enemy's goal is for us to believe the lie. Believing in God's Word gives us the ability to walk in the strength and greatness that was bestowed upon us before we were born. It took a long time and tremendous soul work for me to get to a place of healing. The unbearable pain of my journey produced a woman, mother, and partner with a heart as beautiful as a precious diamond and a healed soul as strong as the platinum it sits in. This super juicy girl deserves all the love and joy God has in this universe and I now relish in all my blessings without apology.

CHRONICLE XI
HEALING COMES AFTER THE HURT

My oldest love dove Perrisse, once asked a great question during one of our frequent conversations. She wanted to know, "Are we ever healed, or is healing a continuous process?" What is healing? We can heal from a non-chronic illness, a scrape on the knee, or a cut on our body. But how do we recover from our emotional wounds, the ones that are deep in our hearts and souls? Healing comes after the hurt when you take the necessary steps to become healthy and whole. The critical point is you must seek help outside of yourself to heal your wounds.

After the dreadful confrontation with Brandon, my suffering was finally apparent to me. The hurting was no longer normal to my mental psyche, and I began to reject the pain. It was time to do my soul work to become emotionally sound and healthy. But I wasn't ready for how difficult and painful the beginning of my healing journey would be. The truth of my trauma was paralyzing; it hurt like hell!

It took a week after the confrontation for the feelings of humiliation and embarrassment to sink into my spirit. *How could I let a man control how I felt about myself?* In full transparency, I felt devastated and lost. I knew I didn't want to be that woman who pined after her husband for the rest of her days. I had witnessed too many women give up on love because they did not, could not, or would not address the love trauma they experienced in their lives.

I know women who never entered another romantic relationship after a bad breakup or divorce. Instead, they buried themselves in their careers, children, or social groups and lived completely alone with no possibility of a love interest in sight. I have even witnessed women who have been divorced for a hundred years but still try to convince their ex to get back together with them. Even worse, some women try to fight the new woman their ex is with!

Although it was easy to empathize with women who chose never to love again, this super juicy girl had to get her healing because I did not want the people who betrayed me to win. My heart and soul would never be restored, and all the people I blamed for my hurt would have gone on with their lives while I lived in a house of pain and unforgiveness. Once I snapped out of the feeling of unworthiness that was on repeat in my mind, it was game on!

The feeling of betrayal led me to anger that I could not control, but that painful house would not be my permanent home. It felt like my relationship had blindfolded me and gently escorted me to the middle of a busy four-lane highway, leaving me alone to make my way to the emergency lane and survive without being murdered by the cars going 80 mph! The attempted murder of my soul forced me into recovery. It was time to heal.

It was time to seek help to discontinue the emotional sabotage that I was inflicting upon myself. Although I suggested that Brandon go to therapy for his irresponsible behavior, he insisted we go to couples counseling. Our marriage was over, and it was no need to do so. I wanted to go to counseling alone to give myself a fighting chance of being transparent about my pain and trauma. I did not want to give Brandon the privilege to have a front-row view of my journey. It was imperative to search for a person who would be culturally unbiased to my pain and childhood experiences.

Feeling a constant sense of betrayal and unwantedness by my parents always haunted me. I hoped that getting married would cure the loneliness that remained in the core of my soul. Since my soul never connected with Brandon, the feeling of being an outsider with the people who were supposed to be my anchors never went away. The core of the brokenness had to reveal itself; it had to come forward if I had any chance of becoming healthy and whole. Someone with an alternative lens needed to guide me through this painful journey; I wanted to go to a counselor with the ability to get where I was coming from without judgment. Therefore, I settled on a counselor who was a Caucasian male, which was completely the opposite of the person I thought I wanted to work with. In retrospect, this was the best decision I made in taking the initial step toward healing.

What was wrong with me? What bad things did I allow to happen? It turned out that I was suffering from something called "love trauma syndrome." Richard B. Rosse, MD, states, "When the loss of love is very distressing, the experience is a love trauma. A love trauma is a form of psychological stress that produces an emotional disturbance that is both severe and prolonged."[2]

Who the hell knew a broken heart was a whole syndrome? How many generations of women have walked around with a broken heart, thought they would get over it, but never did? I witnessed the women in my family do this. As a young girl, I listened to stories of my great-grandmother, who never got over the loss of her relationship with her husband. I remember feeling as if something was wrong with that. A feeling of sadness and empathy came over me as I thought, *why didn't she just move on*

---

[2] Richard B. Rosse, *The Love Trauma Syndrome: FREE YOURSELF FROM THE PAIN OF A BROKEN HEART.* Perseus Publiching, *1999, 1*

and find someone else? I now understand that some people can develop more than the relationship blues. I discovered it was not that easy for some people to get over heartbreak in my research.

When Brandon made his confession, I knew I would never be in a relationship with him again. However, I wanted to take the steps with Brandon to accept the separation without any drama. Although he believed we could work through the issue, I knew we did not love each other. He was only trying to hold on to me as his wife, not as his woman.

What was the difference? As Brandon's wife, I kept his house clean, cooked his food, had sex with him when he wanted, and raised his son. As Brandon's woman, he would protect and provide for his family without question. He would love me and care about my well-being. He would show me his heart and affection. However, he was unwilling to make any sacrifices for me. He was unmotivated to take on the role of being my man; it was not important to him to make me feel safe. When we were away from each other, he did not even call to check on me to make sure I was okay.

"Love trauma does not only apply to romantic relationships. It can happen between parent and children, siblings, and close friends."[3]

[3] Rosse, Richard B. *The Love Trauma Syndrome: FREE YOURSELF FROM THE PAIN OF A BROKEN HEART.* Perseus Publiching, 1999, 12

I promise you; the heavens opened before me when I discovered this fact. Suddenly, all of my traumatic relationships and trauma bonds began to make sense. The continuous loveless relationships with men were merely manifestations of the love trauma I experienced growing up.

As I said before, there were little breaks along the way to set up my downfall; the life-shattering heartbreak that led me down the path to my loveless relationships was the high school graduation day incident. The love trauma I endured should have killed me, and I am entirely sure that is when the enemy made the attempt to murder my soul. The keyword is "attempt" because God was always present and would not allow the enemy to take me! God kept me the entire time until He knew his child was ready to live in her strength and heal from all the wounds inflicted upon me for many years.

In therapy, my counselor focused on my childhood, specifically my relationship with my parents. For the first time ever, I did not feel any guilt for expressing my sincere feelings of hurt and betrayal. It was the first time someone acknowledged that my experiences were not typical; they were not something I needed to "get over." It is my opinion that telling someone to "suck it up" is the worst thing you can do when that person trusts you enough to share their pain.

Leaving my initial counseling sessions, my soul stung with excruciating pain. It was so bad that I had to have an accountability partner to call after each session to make sure I didn't do something stupid, like sleep with someone or eat an entire pizza. My emotions were so raw from reliving the trauma that it felt like I needed a fix. Bless my cousin, Krissie! She held my hand through this initial process. She identified how counterproductive my actions would be and awesomely stood in the gap for me. Because of her, I was able to power through and deal with my issues head-on. Before I knew what was wrong with me, I baked and ate an entire cake, which was indeed my drug of choice during my marriage. After Brandon's confession, I never ate a whole cake again.

Even though counseling was the first step in my healing journey, it wasn't enough. In place of going out and conquering every man I could find to prove that I was still desirable as a woman, I decided to jazz up my super juiciness. I needed to add some pizzazz to my already beautiful self. Yes, this super juicy girl went out and got some new hair, started going to the gym, and began to love herself. Becoming a skinny mini was not in my cards, so working with what I had was more important.

I needed to look and feel good in all of my super juicy glory. One of my besties, Violet, encouraged me to be more confident and not shy away from my greatness, so I began walking with my chin up and shoulders back. Having women in my life who loved and cared for me makes a difference. My friend, Mel, decided to have a destination wedding in Hawaii and planned the trip the week of my birthday. A few of our other sisters also agreed to go, and there we were in beautiful Hawaii on my birthday. Something my soul needed badly. Counseling was working, but the love of my sister circle was a healing that needed to come forth at that time in my life. On top of all that sister love, there was this nice chocolate drop at our hotel on my birthday, and lord behold, this man walked right up to me, introduced himself, and asked for my number! Can we say it was a *Stella Got Her Groove Back* kind of moment!

Yes, Lord!

Won't He, do it?

With the help of counseling, I began to normalize love and joy in all aspects of my life. I wanted to break the cycle of suffering in my family and create loving, safe relationships with my child and my nieces, nephews, and godchildren. Now that my parents are older and romanticize the relationship between us, I can lead by example by behaving respectfully towards them in front of my love doves. My parents profess their love for me, which leaves me feeling torn about allowing myself to be vulnerable and unguarding my heart to them again.

It seems they expect that I leave that part of our lives in the past, forgive the hurt and trauma they caused, and move forward without resolve. This means giving in to the old-school bullshit of sucking it up or sweeping the hurt feelings under the rug. Hiding my pain wasn't working for me anymore; protecting my heart was my new normal, and that was the behavior I began to model for myself regardless of anyone else understanding my position.

The healing is, I fully understand the pathology of the relationship with my parents and fellowship with them when I feel strong enough to endure whatever comes my way while in their presence. I used to go around my mother and father believing my heart was safe only because they were my parents. I thought *This is where I belong.* Then, boom! Heart shattered.

Forgiveness is not all rainbows and unicorns. Finding the strength to forgive myself for taking this strict position with my parents was a task in itself, and it was more challenging than leaving my husband. Healing is a process that comes in different forms, and I didn't have the privilege to discuss my issues with the people who said they loved me in a way that soothed the hurt; I had to find alternative outlets.

Professional counseling and exercise worked for my healing journey. Others may prefer to talk with a church pastor, but healing isn't one size fits all. People are in pain for a myriad of reasons. An important issue for one person may not be as important for the next. Counselors have training and insight into an array of issues that people face. This may be an excellent place to start to get a handle on your pain and trauma. Others may prefer to go it alone or work through their healing process using self-help books and activities. The information highway of the Internet has so many resources available at your fingertips. Search engines give you so many options to utilize without leaving your house. Don't underestimate how helpful books, audiobooks, YouTube videos, and self-help documentaries can be in helping to soothe your soul.

Another resource that was extremely helpful in my journey was music. I cannot live without music: worship songs, R&B, rap, neo-soul, jazz, etc. Music is a true healing source for my soul. Most days, you can't tell me I'm not Aretha, Gladys, Israel Houghton, The Isley Brothers, Mary J. Blige, Leela James, CHIKA, Musiq Soulchild, Kindred and the Family Soul or Lizzo. Shoot, in my mind, I can give Jazmine Sullivan a run for her money, especially when I'm in my car alone with the volume on max. As a young girl, I always said, "If I could sing, I would be rich and famous." The truth is, I can't hold a note to save my life. But I could care less. I sing to heal my soul, and it truly works for me.

Leaning on your faith can also be a great healing place. No matter your religion or belief, it is healthy to look to a higher power to guide your spirit in the right direction. It can be helpful to quiet your mind for spiritual direction. I am a woman of faith; when I accepted God as my Lord and Savior, I began to lean on Him heavily for guidance, especially when I was in my darkest place. The Bible is my friend. When there is no one to talk to, I can always pick up the Bible to help me through.

In addition, journaling can be just as healing as any other resource. When the confrontation with Brandon happened, I began to journal as a way to talk to God. All of my entries began with "Dear Lord." My feelings of anger and humiliation were so great that I felt I could not talk to anyone. When I spoke to my girlfriends, I felt a great sense of embarrassment. I felt a slight level of separation from my core friends, whose husbands were also close with Brandon. Journaling made me feel like I was sitting in God's lap and having a conversation. God is a good listener; He allows you to get it all out with a peace that will heal all hurt and pain.

Uncovering the root of my pain helped me in my journey to healing. For a long time, I only pulled the weeds that showed up at the surface. Becoming a mother brought me to a place of love, which allowed me to dig deep and see that love is possible in all aspects of my life. In the depth of my brokenness, I discovered I was worthy of love and belonging. I took the steps I needed to take to begin living without feeling the hurt of my past trauma. When I feel vulnerable, I take a moment to breathe, push through my fear of rejection, and find love in the situation.

When someone hurts my feelings, I don't accept the hurt or disrespect. Instead, I approach my emotions from a position of strength and take a step back to ensure I take care of my heart and that my soul is intact. When I am ready to speak my peace, I do my best to be honest, and kind, without sugar coating my feelings.

God's love was the primary guide in this super juicy girl's healing journey. I want to encourage you to find what works for you. The healing comes after the pain when you trust your gut and take it one step at a time. Only love bonds are allowed.

CHRONICLE XII
BELIEVING GOD'S LOVE WAS WORTH THE HEALING JOURNEY

1 Corinthians 13:1-13 (NIV)

1 If I speak in the tongues of men or of angels, but do not have love, I am only a resounding gong or a clanging cymbal.

2 If I have the gift of prophecy and can fathom all mysteries and all knowledge, and if I have a faith that can move mountains, but do not have love, I am nothing.

3 If I give all I possess to the poor and give over my body to hardship that I may boast, but do not have love, I gain nothing.

4 Love is patient, love is kind. It does not envy, it does not boast, it is not proud.

5 It does not dishonor others, it is not self-seeking, it is not easily angered, it keeps no record of wrongs.

6 Love does not delight in evil but rejoices with the truth.

7 It always protects, always trusts, always hopes, always perseveres.

8 Love never fails. But where there are prophecies, they will cease; where there are tongues, they will be stilled; where there is knowledge, it will pass away.

9 For we know in part and we prophesy in part,

10 but when completeness comes, what is in part disappears.

11 When I was a child, I talked like a child, I thought like a child, I reasoned like a child. When I became a man, I put the ways of childhood behind me.

12 For now we see only a reflection as in a mirror; then we shall see face to face. Now I know in part; then I shall know fully, even as I am fully known.

13 And now these three remain: faith, hope and love. But the greatest of these is love.

This is the same chapter in the Bible that my mother read to me the night before my high school graduation. Today, I believe every word the Apostle Paul said. After beginning my healing journey, I saw the joy and happiness my mother wanted for me as I was preparing to embark upon adulthood. My light was so bright, and the powerful prayers of my mother were so strong that the enemy did everything in his power to keep me from my destiny. At eighteen years old, what God wanted for my life was already in play, but I did not see it.

My mother had insight into my life path, knowing her daughter possessed the qualities needed to achieve all the goals I had hoped for. Looking back, she more than likely thought that I should have the ability to overcome adversity because she did. Due to distance, she had no idea I had chosen the wrong path and let the distractions of the enemy invade my life; I did not know how to cry out for the help and guidance my life warranted at the time.

There is no need for any shoulda, coulda, woulda. My decisions led me to a life full of love and blessings, and the journey it took to get here was worth it. We must reinforce this message throughout our lives because learning to trust God for everything will save us from the things we can't see when it gets dark, and our vision becomes blurred; I am living proof. Yes, you will be distracted and unsure. The road will be rough, and you will want to quit. But, as Beyoncé says in her song "Freedom," "A winner don't quit on themselves."

I would tell my eighteen-year-old self to love God because He will show you how to love yourself. Believe in God's Word, no matter what, and allow it to guide you when you are lost and confused. More importantly, I share these words with my love doves in hopes that they do not make the same mistake of ignoring God's Word or not loving themselves. I have done my best to live in front of them as a healthy example. I encourage them to identify the tricks of the enemy and anticipate his presence.

The Bible states in John 10:10, "The thief comes only to steal and kill and destroy; I have come that they may have life and have it abundantly." (NIV). In addition to loving us, God also wants us to have abundant lives. Expressing this to young people is a good thing. Offering them resources and guiding them as they learn to utilize this skill should be done more often. My mother was an ordained minister who served in the church and dedicated her life to this work, but I still missed the message she was pointing out to me that fateful night in her hotel room. The next day, I mistakenly chose the enemy and not the Word of God.

For this reason, I don't leave my child uncovered. This world is cruel and will eat our children alive. When children are left to their own devices, they make unsafe choices. Even as young adults, it isn't easy to judge your surroundings as healthy or safe. People, in general, will remain loyal to the allies they grew up with or have done a good deed for them, even if that person has evolved into someone who does not care about them anymore.

I honestly believe that the manifestation of my relationship trauma could have been worse during this time of stupidity if I had chosen to smoke, drink alcohol, or do drugs. Even though the enemy was doing everything possible to snatch my soul, my mind was always clear enough to escape the most ominous situations that were around me. My parents left me unprotected, and I had the wounds to prove it.

My independence did not allow me to call out for them to save me when I connected myself to so many toxic people. I suffered these situations not knowing which way to turn, and the enemy succeeded in convincing me that I was unworthy and unwanted. My life experiences inspire me to be present and available to my love doves whenever they need to talk or vent. I am their sounding board no matter how bad the situation is or how disappointed I may be in their actions. I lead with love always, and they need to know it even in their moments of confusion and uncertainty.

Listen! Expressing love does not always come without caution. It was not something I was able to do simply due to fear of rejection. There have been many times even after my healing journey that my heart was bursting with love, but I could not express it in any way because I was scared out of my mind that it would not be reciprocated. Instead, I let the feeling pass and replaced it with emptiness. Why is expressing love so complicated? I mean, there have been over a million songs written about love. The word "love" appears in the NIV version of the Bible 551 times![4] In 1 Peter 4:8 it states, "Above all, love each other deeply because love covers over a multitude of sins" (NIV). My sister, Phyllis, recited that verse often while we were growing up, but I never paid her any mind because it was just something she said. My heart was so wounded during that time in my life that I missed her message. I always heard people say that "love hurts," so I believed this backward message.

Do we fear love because we fear the unknown? We do not know or understand so much about love; we run from the one thing that God wants us to have in our lives above anything else. Having the courage to lead with love could make any situation tolerable for all parties involved. Understanding love and becoming familiar with the different types of love can help us better navigate situations, people, and relationships. How old were you

---

[4] Reference Staff Writer. "How Many Times Does "love" Appear in the Bible?" (Reference, 26 March 2020.)

when you learned there was more than one kind of love? Do you know there are eight types? I have mishandled several people and relationships by placing them in my limited love box because I only knew about agape love and romantic love growing up.

According to the ancient Greeks, there were eight types of love. The first is Eros (romantic love), in which you would be in a passionate relationship with someone you are intimate with. I can admit since my healing journey, I have been closer to this type of love than I have ever been before in my life, and it feels incredible to love someone this deeply. Philia is (affectionate love) which relates to friendships and family with whom you are on the same page; you get along in many situations and care deeply for the person. I am blessed to identify the people in my life who genuinely care about my well-being and honor our relationship with reciprocity. The third is Agape (selfless love) or God's love.

This is the love I lead within my life and something that I believe we all can practice. It is important to me to have selfless love for everyone that I associate with in my life, regardless of the type of relationship. Storage (familiar love) is also between friends and family. We sometimes connect to other people because they feel familiar based on a memory of someone in our lives. This is another reason why I connected with Brandon. Something was familiar about him, which was comfortable. However, being comfortable with someone should not be the sole reason why you should marry a person. It may work for others, but it did not work for me.

Mania (obsessive love) is a love that is important to control. It can become overwhelming or even scary for the person it is directed towards. When I like a person, I have to talk to myself to ensure I am not obsessing over them. It can be easy to want to possess someone you love. My mother used to tell me that I am not a witch, and I should not try to control how a person feels.

Ludus (playful love) is a love that we should incorporate in many of our relationships. Sometimes parents are so firm with their children, which in most cases is warranted. However, it is okay to be playful and have fun with our children, especially as they get older. It is healthy to maintain a playful side in your romantic relationships as well. Laughing and loving is good for the soul. Pragma is (enduring love) and is a love that I strive to have with my love doves and current romantic relationship. Long-lasting love is important, and it takes work. I now have the courage to lean into love, and I am willing to do the work to maintain healthy, loving relationships that fill my heart with joy.

The eighth type is Philautia (self-love). It is my belief that this goes hand in hand with agape love.[5] The long road to loving myself was worth every step! When you love yourself, it is easier to love others. We should consistently practice self-love in our own lives and encourage our loved ones to do the same. I am grateful to my mother, affectionately nicknamed "Peaches." She was the first to introduce me to God's love, and I now stand in my healing because I understand the different types.

Trusting my gut has helped me to properly place people and relationships in my life. It has helped me accurately identify whether someone is a part of my tribe. If not, I know how to politely place them where they belong in my heart or remove them altogether. When I interact with others, it is easy to notice if they are leading with love. If they are not, I make the necessary adjustments to protect my heart and soul. I have come a long way since the beginning of my healing journey. Recovering from the hurt and shame of my decisions has helped me achieve the goals that I set for myself. I live my life full of "faith, hope, and love. I no longer carry the feeling of unworthiness that burdened me for so long.

Finally overcoming the self-doubt, I developed as a teen gives me the ability to go after what I deserve. The old saying goes, "Closed mouths don't get fed." Having

[5] GCT. "The 8 Ancient Greek Words of Love" (Greek City Times, 14 Feb 2020.)

the courage to open my mouth to assert my needs confidently, professionally, and personally has corrected the trajectory of my life back to a life of purpose. The self-assurance I now possess reminds me that there is no limit to what I want to achieve, and I am shooting for the stars! As I come to the close of the story of my healing journey, I want to leave you with a letter I wrote to my mother, who passed away before publishing this book.

Dear Peaches,

It was because of you that I know, without a shadow of a doubt, what God's love truly is. When I showed you the illustration of my book cover, I had no idea you would not be here to read the finished version of my healing journey. I prayed it would be the catalyst to work on our relationship and bring us closer together. Because of your fervent prayers and belief in the Word of God, I am still here to tell my story. The night you read the Bible to me on the eve of my high school graduation, I left you the next morning feeling like I could conquer the world. Your desire for me to succeed was more present than I had ever seen.

As I write this, I can see your smile. I can feel your heart, and I remember the joy that filled the room with all the hopes and dreams you had for my life. The light in your soul was so bright that I can still see the sun in the room at this moment. I was excited and ready to live up to all that you hoped for in my life, not knowing the enemy was present and would come against me the very same day.

My journey was long and painful, but the trials and tribulations and the protection of our God made me strong. This same strength caused us to have a tumultuous mother-daughter relationship from time to time, but I also know that your prayers, power, and faith made me the resilient woman of greatness I am today. You presented so many lessons about what to do in life. You were my first role model, and I am blessed that all your examples and lessons came full circle on the Easter Sunday, I learned you slipped away.

Ma, I miss you and will hold on to the love you had for me and my son. Knowing now that you suffered and endured so much trauma in your own life with such style and grace, I will live my own life the way that you and God intended with love, joy, and happiness. Even in the midst of our turmoil, you told me as often as you could how much you loved me. You made it plain that you loved your children and the only man you married; you never wavered.

The steadfast love you had for my father paid off. He stood in the gap for us when you passed. He shared wonderful stories about your relationship and how much he loved you. He also made sure you were laid to rest where you wanted to be. I will always be grateful to him for doing that for us, and it also reinforced in my heart that love conquers all.

I wish we had more time. Knowing you are present in my soul and seeing your face every day when I look at myself in the mirror will have to be enough to get me through. I am committed to living in gratitude because my healing journey led me back to putting God first and the memory of your unconditional love will keep me.

Love you fervently,

Your Sunny

CITATIONS

Amer-Marie. "Are You Really In Love Or Just Trauma Bonding?" XO NECOLE, 21 Nov. 2020, xonecole.com/traumabonding/

GCT. "The 8 Ancient Greek Words for Love" Greek City Times, 14 Feb. 2020, greekcitytimes.com/2020/02/14/the 8-ancient-greek-words-for-love/amp/

Knowles, Beyoncé. Lyric to "Freedom." Performed by Beyoncé, Sony Music 2016 LEMONADE).

The Holy Bible, New International Version®, NIV® Copyright © 1973, 1978, 1984, 2011 by Biblica, Inc.® Used by permission. All rights reserved worldwide.

Rosse, Richard B. *The Love Trauma Syndrome: FREE YOURSELF FROM THE PAIN OF A BROKEN HEART.* Perseus Publishing, *1999.*

Staff Writer. "How Many Times Does "love" Appear in the Bible?" Reference, 26 March 2020, reference.com

Lightning Source UK Ltd.
Milton Keynes UK
UKHW021815031222
413218UK00003B/45/J

9 780578 856216